Going to the
Dogs

Additional titles from Finn Cara Press:

Birdsong
by Patricia C. Wright

Tale of the Reed: A Journey of Retreat
by Richard D. Wright

Going
to the
Dogs

RICHARD D. WRIGHT

Finn Cara Press
Derby Line, Vermont

Finn Cara Press

433 Main Street
Derby Line, Vermont 05830

Front cover (*left to right*): Liam, Rowan, and Molly
Back cover: Richard and Molly

Author: Richard D. Wright (1933– 2012)
Title: Going to the Dogs
Includes preface and postscript by Patricia C. Wright, prelude, afterword, biographical note
Subjects: Dogs—Sheepdog, Shetland

ISBN 978–0-9600949-2-9

Printed and bound in the United States of America

Contents

Preface   1

Prelude   3

1. Puppyhood   11

2. Middle Puppyhood   39

3. Late Puppyhood   49

4. Early Adolescence   64

5. Middle Adolescence   78

6. Late Adolescence   89

7. Young Adulthood   104

8. Maturity   127

9. Old Age   139

Afterword   159

Postscript   163

About the Author   165

Preface

WHILE DICK was still teaching, our two collies, Sean and Brigit, were primarily my companions and were mostly cared for by me. Sean was Dick's great gardening companion during the summers, and after his retirement Dick was able to spend more time with Brigit during her final months. But our time with these collies did not prepare us for what would happen next. This is Dick's chronicle of the experience of raising three stubborn, opinionated, and totally adorable shelties from their arrival at nine weeks old to the passing of the last one almost sixteen years later.

During this time we held regular classes in spiritual studies at our home in Vermont, and our dogs came to participate in these as in everything that we did, so that this book also chronicles the experience of often working concurrently with both the dogs and the human students.

Prior to this account, Dick wrote *Tale of the Reed*, centered on one of the retreats led by Pir Vilayat Inayat Khan at the Abode of the Message in New Lebanon, New York, and some of the ramifications of a formal retreat experience.

Through the retreat process one hopes to be led to deeper spiritual insight and understanding. There are many forms of retreat, often solitary—or silent if within a group setting, but *Going to the Dogs* describes what came to be thought of as an almost sixteen-year retreat in everyday life in the care and company of three sheltie dogs.

Preface

The italicized sections of the book are, except as noted, excerpts from letters Dick wrote to family and friends.

This is the background. Now on to the tale . . .

Patricia C. Wright

Prelude

WE HAD not set out to get puppies, not even one. We simply took a drive on a clear fall day. A newspaper advertisement for a litter of collie puppies for sale provided us with an excuse for heading into the countryside to enjoy the fall colors and put aside the difficulties of a hectic week.

Two years earlier the second of our beloved collies, Brigit, had died of complications of old age after a period of intensive care, and still the loss cut deeply. Our first collie, Sean, had been of championship quality and perfect in every way. He was eight weeks old when he came to us from Leon Perry in nearby Brownington, and after Sean made one accidental wet indoors and Pat brought it to his attention, he was completely housebroken. He had superior intelligence, always listened closely when spoken to, and became Pat's best buddy. At each of the two places he came to call home, he required only one walk around the property lines to learn never to go beyond them unless one of us went with him. From the very beginning he understood commands immediately and was a trusted partner in all our activities, including play, and during our educational and dowsing adventures he led us to some of our finest teachers.

In 1977 we went to our first dowsing convention in Danville, Vermont. Sean went with us, of course, and through him we met Terry Ross, then president of the American Society of Dowsers, a man who loved collies. Terry became our primary dowsing teacher and several years later asked us to help him to create a new kind of dowsing school based on mind reach. Terry and I taught that school for four years, and we later wrote its contents into a book, *The Divining Mind*, published by Inner Traditions International. Pat was a field instructor in those schools, and she and I organized the four-day national conventions that followed the schools for the final three of those four years. Included were symposia on Dowsing and Consciousness, Dowsing and Planetary Consciousness, and Dowsing and Creativity. Those offerings in the mid-1980s attracted each year close to a thousand participants, including medical and scientific professionals from a number of countries. Later Pat and I wrote *The Divining Heart* as a sequel to *The Divining Mind*, incorporating some of the material gleaned from those years.

Sean was our dear companion and we wanted what was best for him, so during his fifth year we felt that he needed the companionship of another dog. That's when we again visited Leon, who had a lively young female collie he had rescued with a group of siblings, all half starved, from former owners. She was already housebroken, and even though she was at first a bit wild and lacked Sean's elegant bearing, we brought her home and named her Brigit in honor of the Celtic goddess. Sean and Brigit took to each other immediately, and they became a good team, Brigit keeping him lively and Sean showing her how to be a good member of the family.

Sean began to exhibit a variety of ailments during his seventh year. Even though Pat took him to a number of specialists and we did everything we could through dowsing, he continued to fail until finally, at the end of his final night with us shortly after his tenth birthday, he died peacefully. The loss of Sean was devastating to both of us, but especially so to Pat.

Sean's final gift to us was his occasional spirit presence, and so we came to understand that he was still okay. He first made his subtle presence known to Pat in our large living room a few days after his passing. She could dowse his location, see his hazy form, and also see the form move when she asked him to move across the room. Right after that vision, her first real indication of life continuing after death, she saw a double rainbow in the eastern sky. From then on we were frequently able to sense Sean's presence.

After Sean's death, for a time we didn't know quite how to relate to Brigit. We had seen her primarily as Sean's companion, and it took some time before we learned to appreciate her for herself and her own unique abilities. During the years that followed, Brigit became increasingly attuned to the subtle realms and taught us much about aspects of the natural world. She could sense earth energies and showed us by her actions where there were lines we then could dowse. She was very aware of spirit presences, both human and animal, and brought them to our attention.

Following our introduction to dowsing we had also become students of Pir Vilayat Inayat Khan of the Sufi Order in the West, later known as Sufi Order International (and now as the Inayati Order). Pir Vilayat's message continued that of his father, Hazrat Inayat Khan—the unity underlying the world's religions, while their diversity was to be honored and studied for what each could teach about relationship with the Divine. With permission we gave classes at our home and established a nonprofit teaching center that has continued to the present time.

Aided by Brigit's sensing of the invisible, we were able to develop our dowsing skills more fully and to add in that way to the depth of material we were able to offer in our center classes.

Although I was still teaching high school English during those years, after three decades I was becoming increasingly disillusioned with the mechanized, behaviorist approach toward education that had been adopted by our local school board, establishing a system of command that left teachers disenfranchised. To my dismay most teachers adopted a rubber-ducky approach and were cheerfully willing to tell each other that they were ready to put their noses to the grindstone, bite the bullet, tighten their belts, give a little, and work a little harder. The system clashed with my growing holistic focus, and so I retired from public school teaching in June 1992, which was just as well, because that was when Brigit's health took a serious downturn, and during her final months she required care around-the-clock until her final moments, when I rested next to her on the floor and held her gently as her heart stopped beating. We laid her body to rest in a grave near Sean's in what had become a small memorial garden in our side yard.

> *(10/10/92) Those of you who knew our collie Brigit might want to know that she left this earth plane on Friday. She was close to age 14. Brigit was a teacher to us in many ways concerning the subtle worlds. Also, in the past 14 months of her impaired health, she taught us much about resilience, perseverance, "walking in the desert" in a state of trust, about mutual cooperation, and about love.*
>
> *We will miss Brigit in ways beyond anything we can express but thank her for all that she has given us—and thank God, who loaned her to us.*

During the next two years various aspects involving our small book and gift shop and our interfaith teaching center seemed to become increasingly less harmonious. For many years we had also remained active in the dowsing society, but while we continued to develop our own skills in a grounded way, the society itself became caught up in the currents of New Age woo-woo. We took our leave from active participation in that group even though we continued to develop our own dowsing interests. Our second book related to dowsing, *The Divining Heart*, was then published, and with the hope that the society might be returning to a more responsible stance, we considered attending their annual convention. Hopes were dashed when we looked through the speaker résumés. One gentleman wrote vaguely that he realized something was missing and had begun "to put things together." Another speaker, blessed with "an inquisitive mind," told readers that she had gone on to higher planes. Another, who may or may not have realized something was missing, was qualified to speak on her topic because she had traveled to Great Britain. We learned that two others "would bring through the latest earth changes," although it was not clear whether they would be doing this alone or with their audience. Another was a Doctor of Being and described herself as "sound around a soaring spirit," evidently like a balloon tearing around and making rude noises while the air escaped. Some other lady assured readers that she would be able to help her group receive collective wisdom because she had lived in a teepee for two years. We put both the program and the convention to one side.

Reading that program reminded me of an earlier incident, when my duties at dowsing conventions included leading morning meditations. During one of them, five minutes or so after the meditation had begun, a not-so-young lady clomped into the hall with her slap-soled New Age shoes and took an additional five minutes to *kerplomp* around the hall to find just the right spot to deposit herself. After she did so, she began to sound as though she was crunching several cough drops with her mouth wide open, although it may simply have been that her false teeth were a bit loose. Another five minutes went by and she arose with great fanfare and sought out another spot to deposit herself, this time about two feet directly in front of me. She spread out her rug while pushing other people out of the way, then assumed a "holy" position and went back to her dozen cough drops. At the conclusion of my portion of the meditation, a helper with several Tibetan singing bowls continued with a brief sound meditation. He had been well aware of the problem and wisely included those piercing gong notes that work like ultrasonic cleansers, but as he began, the lady in question again elaborately rearranged herself, prostrated herself toward what she imagined to be her sacred direction, and writhed around in ecstasy amid further crunching sounds while mooning the musician.

By that time we had been leaders of our spiritual study center for over ten years under the aegis of Sufi Order International, and although the classes went well and attracted a variety of people, our center had begun to experience growing pains. Some members wanted meditation practices and discussions to be more strict, while others would have preferred that we dance off in all directions.

It seemed time to revise our focus—not discard the things we were doing but to find another activity that could help to create a balance, one that we could perhaps think of as an ongoing retreat in everyday life. That may have been why, after that particularly hectic week, a trip to a collie kennel had seemed a good excuse to get out and about for an afternoon. The newspaper ad said that the breeder had a number of six-week-old pups. Even though they were all friendly, cuddlesome, and cute, they did not "call" to us and we decided to wait. We talked to Leon.

"You know," he said, "you folks should think about getting a sheltie. I much prefer them to collies. They're loveable, quick to learn, sensitive, and you save ever so much on their food." He then told us that a friend of his, Eugene, had two of the cutest sheltie puppies he had ever seen and we should go look at them. We did, and when we arrived we were greeted by a happy, roiling bumblement of four adult dogs and three, not two, puppies, all littermates. Both sheltie parents were cheerful and bursting with healthy enthusiasm, and the puppies were of course even cuter than Leon had led us to believe. Brigit had required being carried by me during her last days, and since we were getting older, we began to think that a smaller dog, maybe a sheltie, might be a good idea. I was taken especially by the female, who cuddled up just so when I held her, and Pat especially liked the tiny one. She said it could be for Muriel, a Canadian friend whose own perky, good-natured sheltie, Laughan, who often stayed with us, had died a short while before.

We returned a second time with Muriel. She was, as we had thought, immediately attracted to the tiny one, but she felt that he would be too much for her to take on. Then the larger male, who until then had mostly hidden behind the couch, began to make more of an impression on Pat, and she got to thinking. We wavered and even made a third visit, when Pat felt that yes, she did like the large male. We were still trying to make up our minds when Eugene called to say that he really had to know what one or ones we wanted, because someone from Pittsburgh was interested in the smallest one. The thought of that little one being bundled onto a plane and banished to Pittsburgh was more than we could bear. We convinced ourselves that it would not be at all nice to separate the pups, so in a moment of sheer madness we said we would take all three. Somehow or other we failed to notice that fall was already upon us, the puppies had had no training, and that we were, for all practical purposes, clueless that we would be spending our next sixteen years going to the dogs.

1

Puppyhood

First Week

SHORTLY AFTER noon on Thursday, October 20, 1994, Eugene brought the three nine-week-old shelties to us in a carrier box. They were fluffy and perfumed and looked worried and totally helpless. Eugene kept hold of the box as we showed him our sprawling century-old house. Decades earlier the house had been made over into three apartments, two in the main section and one in the adjoining smaller section. A while after we moved in, we made the downstairs apartment in the main section into a shop, selling new and used books, fine crafts, and gifts, and its back kitchen behind the checkout counter would now become the daytime location for the puppies. The upstairs apartment would continue to be used for Pat's textile work. The apartment in the smaller section adjoining the shop had four rooms, with a dining room and kitchen on the first floor and a bedroom and what had become my study on the second floor. Attached to that apartment through the kitchen was a full-sized barn that we had renovated into a large living area with a central wood stove and picture windows facing south. We told Eugene that during the night the puppies would stay in my study, and during the day they would be with me or Pat in the kitchen behind the shop. We explained that we'd accustom them little by little to the big living room in the redone barn area, where we would start them out in a small area. They were not housebroken, and my upstairs study and the disused back kitchen were two rooms that still had linoleum on the floors and could most easily be made puppy-proof. Eugene told us that the dogs were too small to take outside in the increasingly cold weather, so we planned to cover floor areas of those two rooms with newspaper for their wets and businesses. One of our first objectives would be to paper-train them. Our experience with Sean and Brigit led us to think that it would not really be all that big a task, and it didn't occur to us to dowse about it. We had also made "dens" for them in each of the two rooms—large cardboard boxes with doorways cut into the side—and each den had little blankets for them to rest on. For toys they would have knotted socks and a hard rubber ball.

Eugene bid them an emotional goodbye. He told us that for their last night with him, he had let all three of them and their parents sleep on his bed. We could understand his feelings about parting with them; all three were unbelievably loveable little puffballs with large, soft eyes. We invited him to drop by to visit them any time, although we somehow knew that he never would.

After he left we carried the puppies to their den in the back kitchen, where they huddled. They hesitantly stepped out only when they had to "go"—apparently they immediately accepted the box as their den, not to be soiled. Pat and I agreed that whenever they "went" anywhere on the bare floor, one of us would stand them by their mess, tap the floor, gently say "no," and then put them on the paper and praise them. We would immediately clean up their messes, of course, and use a white vinegar solution to scrub the spots they had used. It all seemed simple.

They had been fed Purina Puppy Chow since they were weaned, so we started with that and decided to slowly phase in whatever seemed better. Each one had an own feeding dish, and during supper that first evening each one sampled from all three, drifting from one to the other. Later we carried the pups one by one into the big living room and put them in a large baby basket. First they spent some time looking around at this strange large room, and then they curled up for naps.

Later we took them, again one by one, up to my study, where I would be staying with them for a while at night. Even though I had covered a large area with newspapers, they still did their wetting and business any old place, after which I cleaned it all up and carried them from the bare linoleum ("No-o-o!") to the paper ("Oh, good dog!"). I then joined them on the floor and talked to them and petted them for over an hour until they finally piled themselves on top of each other in their den and went to sleep.

The puppies came in three sizes. The largest one, whom we named Rowan Og (in honor of the sacred mountain ash tree, with the Gaelic term *og* indicating "young"), weighed a little over six pounds. We noticed from the very beginning that when anything new occurred (and at that stage everything was new), he would sit back and study it out. He also struck us as being the quickest learner and the one most responsive. By the end of that first afternoon and evening he knew what the paper was for and would head for it. The middle one, who was clearly a Molly (Pat held that her name was Molly Bloom, although I felt that Molly Og was more fitting, which showed how little I knew), weighed five pounds and had the thickest coat. She had a sweet, gentle nature but also seemed rather bossy, which Pat later came to call her Mae West side. We noted that when the three of them were in a great turmoil of play and showed signs of stopping, Molly would be the one to egg the other two on. We named the smallest one Liam Mor (with the Gaelic *mor* for "big") in honor of our favorite piper, Liam O'Flynn, even though our Liam weighed only a bit over three pounds and was clearly the pesky kid brother despite the three being littermates. He was also the most cuddlesome and appeared to be the most delicate even though during the first evening he had been the last to settle down. Whenever we gently reprimanded him, he put on his "crushed" look and gazed at us with those big soft eyes.

During their first full day in the back kitchen they felt comfortable enough to cut loose, making up games of "chase" and "corner" and "attack" with what seemed to be definite rules, during which they took turns being the one chased or cornered or attacked. Whenever they were more subdued, they went into their den, curled up in a heap, and chewed on each other before settling into a snooze. They ate their meals with hesitation—it was all still new and scary, especially without their parents around—and after each meal they returned to their boisterous games. The books we had consulted said that they should rest after eating, but they didn't know that.

During the early evening we again carried them into the big living room and placed them in their baby basket, where they snoozed as we watched a movie. Once they were upstairs in my study, they chased each other around the room, stopping only long enough to wet and do businesses. About 9:00 I put them into their den, where they tussled and roiled about. Out they came, and they continued tussling and roiling for another hour. Then they, and I, slept until 1:30. That was when they had to come out once more to attend to wetting, after which they returned to their den and I to my bed, at least until 4:30, when they again decided they needed to wet and do even more businesses. More cleanup, and then they played wildly until 5:15, when they returned to their den for a nap. At 6:30 I carried them to the back kitchen for a session of before-breakfast wild play, which they especially enjoyed when I joined in to play "finger" or "tussle" until the arrival of breakfast. Afterward they again piled together for a snooze.

By the second day Liam clearly knew what the paper was for. My guess was that he was tired of looking crestfallen every time we pointed to his mess and said "No-o-o!" Molly was still the independent one and showed no intention to wet or do her business where her brothers had already done theirs, preferring to choose the cleanest, tidiest spot she could find, preferably off the paper. We decided to cover any wet papers with more paper and just pick up droppings as soon as they appeared, regularly scrubbing the area with white vinegar solution and putting down fresh paper.

By the end of the third day Molly decided to use the paper, and every time she did we praised her. The only problem with all three was that if they became distracted by play, they would wet any old place, but even so, it was our innocent belief that they might just possibly be catching on.

Even though they hadn't yet caught on to their names, they began to feel at ease with us. If I left them even for a brief time, when I returned they all pranced about and wiggled their greetings, whereupon I would crouch down, drum my fingers on the floor, and mix in with them.

We had the notion that they might learn more quickly to use the newspapers if they were kept separate from each other during the day, but then we worried that they might become lonely. On the one hand, their being together kept them active, but on the other hand it also kept them distracted from learning much of anything. Whenever they cut loose and roughhoused, they forgot about not running on damp papers or barking hysterically and it would be back to saying "No-o-o!" and holding the wildest of the three for a while. By the end of the third day I was beginning to wonder if they would ever learn to be housebroken, especially since it was already three times longer than it had taken Sean to learn.

Pat now began to ease their diet away from commercial dog food, adding a bit of cottage cheese and cooked rice to the meals. The dogs thought these were quite nice and ate them first thing.

That third evening we didn't take them into the living room with us. Instead, we left them in the back kitchen, where they listened to Vivaldi and dozed. Afterward I went back with them and wrote a letter before taking them upstairs, the idea being that they would then be more ready for bed. Even so, once they were upstairs they again romped with no sign of settling down. First I tried holding each one separately, but that didn't work so I tried sitting by their den, outstaring them, patting their blanket, and saying "Lie down!" It took a while, but it worked. Then about 12:30 Rowan whimpered and had to be lifted out to wet, which got the others going. After more urging they again settled down until 4:15, when they all had to wet. Shortly afterward Pat got up, which meant that they were sure that it was time for me to get up too. They wiggled a greeting and all did businesses, then they tussled and cavorted until I picked up Rowan, who settled down in my arms as the others drifted back into their den. I put Rowan with them and took Liam onto the bed with me, where he stretched out on my stomach. When the others were quiet, I put him back in the den and they all curled up together until about 7:00.

Rowan had become the first greeter whenever Pat or I left and then returned to the room. He was also the one that especially liked to be fussed over. He had discovered that if he did anything slightly naughty, like chew on the linoleum, he would be held, which may have explained why he continued to do slightly naughty things.

Liam was now the one that had to be watched for his own good. About midmorning of the fourth day he ran under the rocking chair and it bit him. There was great screeching, both at that moment and afterward. I held him for quite a while, and he looked totally mournful even though nothing hurt anymore and a close examination of all body parts showed him to be in good shape. Even so, I held him until shortly before lunch. There was a delayed reaction, though. Near the end of lunch, in the middle of a last bite of food, he jerked away, trotted to the den, sat, and shivered more and more out of control. I held him, but he couldn't stop shivering for nearly an hour. I took him to my study and lay down with him while he snoozed. Pat then stayed with him while I made coffee and checked the other two. The reaction did pass, and when we returned him to the back kitchen, he was ready for another round of romping and tussling.

Their adjustment to a change of diet took time, and even with mixing the cottage cheese and cooked rice with Puppy Chow, their businesses during the day were copious but soft. We held on to the thought that with slow but steady changes in diet their systems would become clear and they would adjust.

The fifth day began with another Liam incident. They had awakened at 4:30, at which time they all dutifully wet on the paper. After they greeted Pat an hour later, they all did their businesses, which I immediately picked up and flushed away. All three then wanted to come onto the bed, where they again romped and tumbled together. I left the bed to attend to a bit of overlooked dropping and Liam decided to jump off. He gave great yelps of pain when he crashed to the floor and again needed more holding and cuddling. The whole episode reinforced our thought that Liam would more than likely be the one who would get into the most scrapes.

Everything was moving along as expected, but the fifth day was a "heavy" late October day, cold and overcast, and we felt stressed by our change of routine. By now we began to suspect that training and tending to three dogs was going to turn into more of a major challenge than we had thought. Two puppies probably wouldn't really have been a problem, but by now I was beginning to realize that three puppies equaled three handfuls and I had only two hands.

By midafternoon all three rose from a nap, tussled about for a while, and then took to wild running and mischief making. Earlier we had weighed them and found that in just five days they had each gained a pound, which meant that even though they still played as they had from the start, they were now heavier projectiles. At one point their play became so wild that I took Liam, the smallest projectile, up to my study for a time out while Pat looked after Rowan and Molly.

It wasn't until 10:00 that evening that they were ready to settle quietly into their den. Earlier Pat stayed with them while I gave the back kitchen floor a good cleaning, put a load of wash into the washer and dryer, got floor papers ready for the next day, and replenished the vinegar solution, all of which made us feel that maybe, just maybe, it all might just possibly be too much, with the constant need to give attention and supervision. It was becoming difficult to abide by the ground rules: no anger, no shouting, keep the "no" simple but firm, give regular praise and assurance, and hold each one for a while by itself. We would have been willing to let them cut loose and explore the house, but we couldn't trust their plumbing or general behavior. The requirements of those five days had taken us by surprise, and something needed to change. Neither of us could leave the dogs alone for more than a few minutes, and there were no more daylong stretches of solitude and study. I wondered how on earth I could now prepare for our weekly center classes. We couldn't even go shopping or anywhere else together. Togetherness was limited to our being with the dogs in the back kitchen or in my study. Was it worth it? At that point we weren't sure, but we hoped it would be. After all, they had only been with us for less than a week.

The next night, after one period of wetting, they rearranged themselves, chewed on one another for a while, and then slept until 6:15, when they woke up in good spirits, and in the back kitchen before breakfast developed a new game called "stare." Two of them some distance apart would eye each other and one would stalk forward. The challenge would be to see which one would break or blink first. They would then roil about and do it all over again.

We also decided to try a new control tactic. After their breakfast, while I showered, dressed, and fixed my own breakfast, I had Liam stay behind, leaving Pat with only two dogs to contend with while Liam padded about, forlorn, in my study.

During that sixth day Rowan began to know for a fact that he liked to be held and would even come to one of us and ask to be picked up. And when the others weren't nearby, he now often curled up by my feet either to stand guard, snooze, or chew away at a shoelace. Molly continued to be the independent one, not at all as helpless and cuddly as she had been when we first saw her, and she didn't particularly like to be held unless she was sleepy. She was still the one who kept things going once they started, the one most out of control during play, and the one then needing the most calming.

The sixth day was also the day when the veterinarian, Doctor Susan, came late in the afternoon to check them out and give them their shots. To our relief she actually listened when we talked about alternative approaches to medical matters, and she later read some of the books we gave her. She even brought along a special vitamin supplement we had wanted to use, one she had ordered with her own credit card. We talked with her about getting the dogs spayed and neutered, but we couldn't resolve that issue. After all, we might decide to breed them with other shelties, and besides, we felt nervous about anesthetics based on an experience with Sean, who, after an operation, had almost failed to come out of what had been minimal anesthesia. We ended up talking with Susan for a long time about dog care, during which time she suggested brands of dog food that were okay and warned us of ones that were junk. She was exhausted from a busy day, but even so, she answered all our questions with patience and good cheer.

Just before she arrived, all three dogs had decided it was time to do huge wets and complicated businesses, which meant that I had to race around cleaning up while Pat greeted her. When she came to the back kitchen, the dogs viewed her with caution, because aside from a short visit from Muriel several days before, no "outsider" had entered the room. Molly and Liam took themselves off to a protected corner, and Rowan came over to me and sat on my shoe. After a while all three piled up around me. During their examination and shot, each one was very good, even though the shot was something new and itched afterward.

We had decided that they should have the full course of standard shots. That first shot would do little besides alert the immune system, which meant that the pups would now be more susceptible to things than they had been and would therefore need to be isolated for another three weeks. If it was dry outside, they could go out for a few minutes at a time, but that would be it. Allowing strangers to come in was a big no. We needed to tell our center class members to stay home if they had colds or sore throats or a pet that seemed the least bit droopy. We also had to keep our shop closed. In three weeks the pups would get their second shots, which would then take an additional two weeks for maximum effect. Then after their third shots, they'd be protected for a year.

When Doctor Susan left, we gave the dogs supper and foraged something for ourselves, even breaking our own training and lifting a glass or two, after which we took the dogs into the living room, put them in their basket, and watched the usual few minutes of news. Later, back in my study, Rowan wanted his independence and refused to stay in the den with the others. Finally I let him out into the room, and he curled up and slept on the floor for about two hours, after which he decided that the den was pretty comfortable and maybe the others weren't such a bad lot after all.

The seventh day turned out to be a bit of a challenge. All three had made the decision that there was no need for newspapers, and they decided to ignore them. Every time one of them "forgot," I gathered all three of them up, tapped the floor by the mess and said "No-o-o!" several times, then turned them toward the papers and said praiseworthy things. After a while they were again okay, but it reminded us that after a week they were still nowhere close to being trained.

By that Thursday they had become a bit like three different kinds of dogs. Rowan had become more like a collie in size and temperament and was developing more independence. Molly was still the chunky little sheltie. Even though she often didn't particularly like to be held, she would hang around nearby whenever she changed her mind. She also continued to be strong-willed. Whenever she began to play wildly, not even holding her would calm her down. Liam was always ready to curl up on my lap, but then he'd be full of activity during the swirl of roughhouse. He and Rowan were now the ones who wiggled all over when they greeted Pat or me.

As a result of that talk with the vet we became more definite about keeping all three away from other people for a while. The positive outcome would be that they would remain in good health. The negative outcome that didn't really enter our minds then was that this would seriously impact their socialization skills. During the afternoon I fixed the front room of the shop for the center class, and that evening began by explaining to the group that the dogs needed to remain isolated for a while, and they all listened. I laid it on so thick about their staying home if they had any colds or upsets, or if they had been around anyone with germs, or if they had droopy pets, that I wondered if any of them would return for future classes.

Second Week

The second week with the threesome started well but then came close to hitting bottom. The problem was not, of course, with the dogs but with our perception of the situation and our degree of fatigue. When their periods of play spun out of control, I was sometimes tempted to grab a newspaper, wave it around, emit a war cry, and indiscriminately start swatting.

Instead I'd pick up the two that were most badly misbehaving and hold them gently but firmly while telling them okay, that's that, now easy, relax. That calmed them, and me, down, and when I put them into their den they'd curled up quietly and snoozed on top of each other.

Pat was still adjusting their diet. Puppy Chow used a corn base, which was proving hard going for them, so following our vet's suggestion she tried One, which had a rice base and was better for their uncertain plumbing. She planned to take Liam mostly off dry food and give him rice, oatmeal, supplement, milk, and carrot or other vegetable. On the eighth day she gave him some of that mix for his lunch, and he finished most of it before he felt the urge to sample the other dog lunches.

That afternoon we put new collars on them, attached leashes, and took them to the backyard. At first they were frightened, and Liam just stood and shivered. Then they realized hey, we're outside, and they began to romp in the leaves. The experience woke them right up, and when we brought them back in they gobbled any leftover lunch and whooped around before taking their naps. Later we took them out again, and after they were back inside I had to leave them for a few moments. I returned to find wetting all over the floor. That's when I lost my cool, shouted "No!" and whacked rolled-up newspaper on the floor and chair. Even though they had no idea why I was upset, they all felt very hurt and crept around, finally tiptoeing over to me, curling up at my feet, and remaining quiet.

By day 9 I again felt that it might well be all too much—not too much to have maybe one puppy but too much to have three. If I supervised one, the other two were invariably causing trouble, and if I simply let them be, they fed on each other's wild behavior. When we woke up in the morning their routine was the usual—early rising, businesses, romping about, a snooze, more romping, and then my taking them downstairs. A new problem was that they would use the papers and then run and tussle about, rolling into whatever those papers had contained or grabbing a business and carrying it around like a toy.

At mealtime Pat now prepared specially cooked meals with supplements individually determined, but since all three were used to eating out of each other's dishes, each meal required constant supervision. After breakfast that ninth morning Pat took Rowan into the front room with her. She had spread papers around, but Rowan decided the only place to wet was on the rug. After she returned him to the back kitchen with the others, the two males briefly napped while I held Molly, who now found that she rather liked it and made herself comfortable. After lunch I took them outside, but this time it was all too much for them and Liam just shook while Rowan huddled against me. Molly shivered and sat down, and when she returned inside, she quickly went to the linoleum and did a bit of everything.

I now began to feel that if this period of time was supposed to shape up as a retreat, so far it didn't seem to be working. Then again, maybe feeling overwhelmed and disappointed was the way a retreat should start.

On the table in the back kitchen I kept a pile of tapes, and every day I played music in the hope that it would keep them a shade more mellow. The pile included five tapes of Vivaldi, three of folksinger Gordon Bok, a longish one of the Pachelbel Canon, a Robbie Gass tape, several of Schubert, a few of drumming, some Irish harp music, and a selection of boozy Irish ballads. For some reason the boozy Irish ballads seemed to encourage them to tussle with each other, while Robbie Gass put them into a stupor.

Even with the tapes, by late afternoon of day 9 three puppies seemed to be three too many, and I was almost ready to call Eugene to ask him to take back the shelties. Then by evening I felt that it would be okay to keep maybe just one and then see to it that the other two went to good homes. The problem was that I couldn't determine which would be the one to keep, so we all went upstairs to settle down and sleep on it.

By the tenth day I knew for a fact that it had become all too much. In the morning we had our annual nonprofit center corporate meeting, which always went all right even though getting the group to agree on anything was a bit like trying to herd cats. The meeting had required preparation as well as focus, and although the dogs had been fairly good, during the afternoon they did eighteen wets and four businesses in just one two-hour period. When the meeting was over, Pat looked after their rampaging while I went outside to rake leaves. Afterward we took them outside again. They decided they didn't want to be led, so we all simply walked or stood around.

During supper we tried to decide what on earth to do next. We knew that they weren't even three months old yet and that we couldn't really expect anything until after six months, but we didn't know whether we were up to at least three more months of puppyhood. By now it seemed clear that we didn't have a clue about how to help them develop plumbing control and have it become a habit or how to break them gently of their more outrageous puppy tussling or how to encourage each one to become a self-possessed member of the household.

That evening, to our relief, they began to redeem themselves, and when we took them into the living room and let them arrange themselves in their carrier, we realized how heartbreakingly lovely they were. Then at bedtime they settled down well and slept until 4:45, at which time I took Liam onto the bed with me while the other two stayed in their den and quietly chewed each other.

On the eleventh day things again fell apart, and by lunchtime first one, then another, started deliberately not using the papers. I would scold one and clean up, during which time at least one of the others would have messed up somewhere else. All this was in spite of constant encouragement, keeping the floor clean, and putting down fresh papers. Later that afternoon, when a friend came over to help me with leaf raking, they continued the same behavior while Pat was looking after them. While Pat fixed their suppers I again tried to supervise. At one point Rowan, obviously in distress, circled about to do business. I put him on the paper with words of encouragement. He struggled to leave the paper. I let him go and he investigated a bare area of the floor. Back I took him to the paper. More struggles. When I let go, he darted across the room, and by the time I reached him he had done a large, soft business on the clean floor. Liam acted much the same, refusing to wet on the papers despite encouragement. He would wet on the floor, crouch against the door to the den, and wait to be scolded. When we took all three to the living room, they refused to settle into their carrier. During their round of final downstairs wets I had to force Liam to stay on the papers, and he held back as long as he could. Despite the congratulations extended while he did finally wet, he still acted defeated.

I was back to the thought that relocating them to good homes with or without payment seemed like a good idea. Pat, however, had given various reasons for their misbehavior: (1) they were only puppies and puppies forget, like babies; (2) we took them outside and the floor is something like the grass and we didn't scold them for wetting on the grass; (3) each one was only establishing its own territory, the way wolves do, and tried not to do stuff on any other territory. Even so, they were still a long way from the popular sheltie image of being trustworthy, sensible, loveable, and intelligent. Well, okay, maybe still loveable.

The next morning, after they were settled in the back kitchen, I tried leaving them alone briefly, but Molly began yapping hysterically. I picked her up and carried her out of the room, but the other two howled so I brought her back. After I left they went back to their roughhousing, and when I returned Rowan looked very subdued, walked with a limp, and yipped every time he put pressure on his left front paw. He had evidently put that paw under the rocking chair just when Molly got it moving. I held him for a while, and when I put him down Liam decided it was time to bedevil him. Fortunately Pat arrived with their breakfast, which they sampled sparingly before they all decided to nap. Rowan, still the subdued puppy, stayed by my feet.

Their continual wetting on bare floor led to a decision that governed the rest of the day: I decided that I would not reprimand them for any "mistakes." What I would do would be to cover every wetting with paper, no matter where it was. A puddle appeared; I covered it, and it soon soaked through. They sniffed it. Shortly thereafter another puddle appeared, this time closer to their den. I covered it, and it too was soon soaked through. They sniffed it, left, returned, sniffed it again. It was still there. Then more wets, but by now they were either on or close to the paper. And so it went for the rest of the day, by which time they were wetting on fresh paper and sniffing with disapproval at any uncovered wettings, which I gratefully accepted as one small step forward.

By day 13 I began to realize that maybe everything so far had been part of a retreat after all and that it might now be the time to give up long-range expectations about their behavior or training—or indeed about our own levels of exhaustion—and just concentrate on what seemed right during any particular moment. It was not the time to worry about what was proper or fair for their upbringing or about the interference in our everyday activities or about the tiresomeness of being on deck. It was a time simply to be, to recognize retreat mode, and try to maintain a single-point focus on the here and now. Winter was approaching, there would be things that needed doing, and the dogs would be shut up all the more, but at the moment it didn't matter. If we stopped to think about it, we'd probably decide all over again that it couldn't be done.

One example of keeping calm and letting things flow occurred at 3:00 that morning. Liam became restless. I got up, put him on the paper, and he wet. By then the other two were restless, so I let them out of their den, during which time Liam did a business. I picked it up, carried it to the bathroom, and flushed it away. By then all three began to howl. I returned, walked over to check their wettings, and stepped into a lake of dog pee. Very calmly I sort of hobbled over to a dry piece of newspaper and put my foot on it. The newspaper soaked up most of the dog pee but it also stuck to my foot. I put my other foot next to it and raised the first one. Then my other foot was stuck.

After getting unstuck I walked sort of on my heels back into the bathroom to wash my feet. By the time I returned, they had all done copious businesses, Liam for the second time. Stepping more carefully, I picked it all up, flushed it away, covered the lake with newspaper, and put them back into their den. They briefly protested but soon decided that they were quite ready to go back to sleep. I was too.

They followed their breakfast with two hours of wild play, and when I sensed that they were ready to quit anyway, I left them to get coffee. They must have thought I was angry with them, because this time when I returned they acted contrite and subdued, as if to say, "We didn't mean to make you mad. If we're good, will you stay?" I did, and they curled up by my feet.

I had also figured out why Liam was becoming so attracted to droppings. It all came clear when I watched him do a business and then take it off the paper and start to carry it away. After I took it from him, I realized that he had been watching me and noting that I always immediately picked up droppings. He hadn't figured out what I did with them, so when he picked them up he just carried them about.

At 5:00, on the morning of day 14, when Pat's alarm went off, all three woke up and tried to get through the door of the den at the exact same moment. Once out, they headed for the papers and simultaneously squatted. I wasn't yet ready to get up, so we all reached a compromise. I was allowed to go back to bed only if I took all three of them with me. They thought that was pretty neat and soon found their spots: Rowan under my chin, Molly down by my hand, and Liam just barely out of reach. They were quiet until about 6:30, when they decided enough was enough and it was time to go downstairs.

By now they were accustomed to my being part of the pack. When we were all in the back kitchen, I purposely wandered out more often so that they would get over thinking "Oh no, he's going, maybe forever!" every time I left. When I was around, they were in training, but whenever I left, they would both howl and revert, wetting hither and yon and tossing papers about.

The three pups had now been with us for two weeks, and we noted the changes. All three were going through growth spurts or body tone spurts or some other kind of spurts. They slept hard, and they played wildly but with better coordination, the males a bit aggressively, which we decided was good. They also now yapped a lot. Rowan was now becoming rather weedy—long and thin. Liam, still the tiny one, ate as much as Rowan and Molly, but he did many more businesses. When they played they didn't bumble as much, and when we returned from being elsewhere they didn't wiggle as much, either, although they greeted us with enthusiasm. They also howled more whenever I left. Along with their becoming more stubborn and willful, they appeared very healthy and good-spirited. The really good news was that the nice lady at our local newsroom took pity on me and agreed to be our source for a virtually unlimited supply of old newspapers, so we could now use them more freely.

Third Week

On the morning of day 15 Pat reopened the shop. By the end of the day she was exhausted and headed for bed. I let the dogs tussle about in the back kitchen until about 9:00 before I took them upstairs for the night. Around 3:00 they had to go onto the papers and do everything. After the males were settled back into their den, Molly decided that she really wanted to sleep on the bed. Then at 4:30 Liam wanted to come up, too. At 6:00 Rowan woke up, paused halfway out of his den, and announced that it was time for everyone to get up.

One change I noted that third week was that they were now much more clever. We had placed cardboard in front of the doorway to the back kitchen, but they learned to push aside the barrier and race happily into the shop. One of them alone couldn't do it, so they combined their efforts. We didn't punish them for it other than saying "No-o-o" and moving them away from the barrier, but finally the easiest solution was simply to give up on the cardboard and shut the door whenever we had to leave them alone.

They were also now more muscular and ready for action, which meant that even though they were willing to roil about noisily but politely, they obviously wanted to be doing other things, although by now it was too cold and rainy to run about with them outside. Whenever their play spun out of control, one of them soon yelped in pain and went limping off, terribly aggrieved, and the one who caused the yipping would feel guilty and lie down. Whoever was left would then find an old slipper, sit down, and chew.

Their appetites had increased, too, and by that third week they finished each meal within minutes while I scurried about refreshing the newspapers. They were particularly attracted to the sections with inserts, first reducing the Grand Union ad to soggy dog pee and then taking on the Revlon special. Later in the week they were drawn to political ads, deciding for whatever reasons to do most of their businesses on the Republican candidates.

During this time they further mastered the skill of sliding the barrier away from the door. Rowan and Molly would hold their claws onto its edge and move it along in unison while Liam supervised. I found it quite impressive and didn't have the heart to admonish them.

Whenever Pat watched them, she said that each one responded to its name and came when called. Whenever I tried it, they responded as though I had made some sort of rude noise best ignored. Pat also had brought a larger box home from the Grand Union to use in the living room instead of the baby carrier. We tried it out briefly before their supper, and they decided that it was some sort of puzzle that they had to solve, after which they could escape.

At bedtime they were fascinated by my change from daytime clothes to pajamas. They leaped about with excitement when I removed my trousers. Maybe they thought I shed my skin. In any case, they tumbled about and wiggled nearly out of control until my pajamas were safely on and they were sure it was okay to go into their den for their first round of sleeping. All except Molly, that is. She would remain seated and give me a look as if to say, "I'm Molly." So I'd put her on the bed, where she then arranged herself somewhere between my kneecap and ankle until the middle of the night, when all three had to tend to business. During one particular night, after their clearing out and my cleaning up, all three of them sat and gave me a look, so all three ended up on the bed, taking up most of the prime space until 6:30, when they all again headed for the papers. Liam's performance was becoming a mystery: he was becoming increasingly chunky even though more seemed to go out one end than went in the other.

Sunday afternoon I installed a baby gate in the doorway to the back kitchen, which they took as a signal for a new game. They found that it left just enough room so that all three could crawl through and go romping into the shop. They were disappointed when I put cardboard backing on the gate, but the open door provided good air flow and did also let them see what, if anything, might be going on in the other room that required their immediate attention.

During Sunday evening heavy wind arrived along with snow that covered the car and the leaves and the roof until midmorning the next day, when it all dripped away, leaving bare trees, soggy ground, and fast moving, heavy clouds with puffy linings. By late morning the sun shone through the little east window over the back kitchen sink for the first time in three days. Liam noticed it especially, because it warmed a square on the floor and he discovered that it was very nice to lie there.

The newspaper inserts continued to praise various political candidates. I had lost track of them but did note that they all promised to reform the government, which was evidently in a terrible mess. I subjected them to a sort of trial by water by putting them on top of dog pee and, just as I had suspected, the conservative candidates soaked it up much better than the liberal ones.

Tuesday, November 8, went routinely well, but Wednesday was two steps backward. After lunch, when we took them out on their leashes for a romp, they all tore about the yard as fast as their leashes and the agility of the two humans permitted. They were in no hurry to return to the house either, and once back, were in no hurry to settle down, remaining beyond the reach of discipline for the rest of the day. If I picked one up, the other two ran wild. They broke off long enough to eat supper, and then it was back to wildness. We tried isolating each one—Molly in my study, Rowan in the living room with

Pat, Liam in the back kitchen. Still no success: Liam messed up the kitchen; Rowan was a ball of energy and fought being held; Molly ran about and scattered papers every which way. I took them all up to my study when they showed signs of running down, but they were at it again until late in the evening.

The next day, day 21, was quieter, perhaps as a reaction to Wednesday's wild reversion, but we felt exhausted from the combination of shop and housework and meals. Concerning the dogs themselves, though, it was all a case of our adjusting to the beasties and being on deck for everything else at all times.

Rowan had grown less thin and scraggly and was now more solid and muscular, but he was also becoming more aggressive, which concerned us. Molly had begun to go from chunky to rangy, and Liam was becoming even chunkier. In many ways he was still the helpless, wide-eyed one, but he could be as tough as nails whenever he took after the others.

We had to remember that they were still heedless puppies, and whenever they played wildly, they wet seemingly dozens of times. During some days we tried taking them to the living room one by one, watching them closely until they seemed ready to do something on the rug, and then returning them to the back kitchen, the main problem being that if we weren't watching them closely, they might all of a sudden squat and let loose.

They also now enjoyed being led around on their leashes. Whenever I walked into the back kitchen wearing my sweater, they jumped and wiggled because that meant we would be going outside. One day, when I was getting ready to head uptown, I made the mistake of walking into the back kitchen while wearing the sweater, and it took me a moment to figure out why on earth all three suddenly seemed to go berserk.

During the night the bed in my study was now becoming their bed. It was rather pleasant having them sprawled around me, but it meant that whenever one of them was restless, I'd have to put that one on the floor to wander aimlessly for a few moments, maybe do a half-hearted wet, and then return to the side of the bed and ask to be lifted back up. Whenever I started to feel annoyed, I reminded myself to think of it as part of an extended retreat.

Fourth Week

The fourth week started with the usual routine—wild play, snoozes, and more wild play. When Pat went to town to shop, the dogs spun into wild mode, and when she returned, she needed to tend to other things connected with supervising a party for a handicapped person the next day. I had hoped that after their day of wildness they'd become calm and serene, but then by the next day things hit the fan.

First came the night, when all three were so restless that by morning I was ready for a good night's sleep and the dogs were ready for another day of fun and games. After Pat left to spend the morning preparing for that party, I took the dogs outside on their leashes one at a time so that each one could run about. I started with Rowan, the large one, and worked my way down through Molly to Liam. It occurred to me that anyone strolling by must have wondered how on earth one large puppy could progressively shrink down to being a teeny thing.

The party Pat supervised ended up being a major trial. The young helper who was to clean the apartment had not done it because she knew for a fact that the hose to the vacuum was hopelessly clogged, and she had already spent two hours trying to get it unclogged. Pat brought it to the house, I took it outside, and ninety seconds later had it unclogged, whereupon Pat returned it to the party location. Then the person for whom the party was being organized criticized Pat roundly because she dared express disappointment to the young helper that the floor was soaking wet from a last minute mopping. More difficult, though, was that despite a number of invitations sent out, only one person showed up all that afternoon, making the whole project a waste of time and energy.

Later that day Kari, the one person who had attended the "party," came to the house to see the dogs, who were briefly on their best behavior. When she left, Pat was worn out and left me with the shop and dogs. Then three junior high age girls came in, full of sass and ginger, and while poking through the store managed to break the glass on a large framed picture. They swore they had nothing to do with it, but there had been a crash and a giggle, and there it was, initially well propped, now flat on the floor, broken. They finally left and I returned to the dogs, who by then had wet everywhere and then cavorted through the large pools of pee, liberally soaking themselves and their toys along the way. They had evidently decided to behave not unlike those three junior high girls.

By late afternoon I felt sick of dogs, shop, and pointless parties. I cleaned up the dog mess and took wild Molly upstairs with me while I lay down for half an hour, taking her back down for her supper. Since Pat had caved in after her hectic day, I stayed with the dogs until they finally slowed down enough for me to think about taking them upstairs for the night. I had to remind myself during this time that it was necessary to take one step at a time, one breath at a time, and harbor nostalgic memories of well-trained collies.

The next day, Sunday, the center class met in the morning with Pat giving the class. The dogs decided to be well-behaved, sleeping or wandering about cutely one at a time. The Sunday classes generally required much preparation, and although group response was good, each session could be exhausting. Sometimes Pat or I asked, "What would the center people do without the class?" Events of the previous few months gave us the notion that they'd do just fine without the class, even though way down deep we knew that the classes really did mean something to them. The classes went on because people gained from them whatever was appropriate for them to gain at the time. It took us a while to reach that understanding, but once we did, we found that the classes became less taxing. We were becoming more aware of one of the themes of our center classes, that things were continuing to unfold behind the scene as they were meant to do despite outward appearances to the contrary. In addition, and aside from the people or the content, our more relaxed attitude may have been influenced by our willingness to let go. Our major focus now was on dogs, and the classes were something to be taken care of around the edges. Whenever one of them was over, there was no time to fuss about it; the dogs required attention. I decided that perhaps that letting go might work with the dogs, too.

The next day we blocked off a section of the living room, spread papers in a new wetting tray, and during the afternoon brought the dogs in and turned them loose. We showed them the tray, but Rowan was the only one who would use it. Molly went close to it but missed it. After their supper we tried watching a light comedy on TV, but it was accompanied by steady shouts of "Rowan, come here" and "Molly, don't" and getting up to stop one of them from doing something and mopping up the rug whenever Molly or Liam wet on it. It wasn't a pattern that lent itself to TV watching, not even for light comedies.

By day 26 their behavior and actions were down to routine variations of Dog Days. We did note that Rowan now enjoyed periods of being Only Dog with Pat and me, although he cheerfully joined in the puppy play. If I were to leave them wherever they were, he was now the one who set up the loudest, most heartrending howl. Molly continued to be the most self-contained, even though she acted less mature than Rowan. She could be by herself with little indication of being upset, but she still didn't seem to have a clue about using the box in the living room. She also was continuing to drag soggy, smelly papers all around the back kitchen for play. When she wasn't being wild, though, she projected the most sense of stillness. Liam, who was becoming even chunkier, had the most "cuteness," like a cheeky but funny little kid. He was also the one to act the most cuddly and helpless when picked up. They were now three months old and as lovely as could be, even though they all still showed stubborn resistance to developing toilet habits.

The next day, Wednesday, started as another routine dog day. After Pat returned from a round of shopping I did take Rowan out, and he ran about on his leash knowing that the outdoors was exclusively his. Pat told me that the other two, especially Liam, put up an almighty howl, asking the world to bear witness to their cruel neglect. They evidently sought revenge by again spreading wet papers all over the floor and stuffing as many of them as possible into their den. When I returned they couldn't imagine why on earth I kept repeating "Oh! Oh!" with a downward fall of the voice.

I noted that whenever they were now in my study, they first wandered around and played a bit. When I prepared for bed they continued to become excited as I shed my skin but they would also now play "foot" with me and try to subdue my toes. Then they roamed until one of the lights was turned off. Liam was usually the first one I put on the bed. Once up, all three would then arrange themselves. They seemed to have caught on that bed meant sleep, and after lights out I'd stretch out while they rearranged themselves.

By the last day of the fourth week they reminded us that they were still in transition. They finished their breakfast and all seemed well, but then everything unraveled. Pat had to leave for an appointment and the dogs decided it was time to cavort. Rowan didn't let either of the others rest. At one point he did a business, moved halfway across the room, and decided he wasn't quite done and deposited a soggy remainder in the middle of the floor. The other two saw the chance to mess about with a dropping and came running. I did a major wipe-up job with one hand while holding off dogs with the other. Then I scrubbed the area. While I was putting away the cleaning material, Liam, upset from strenuous playing, threw up on the same spot. Again the others came running, and again I fended them off with one hand while taking care of the new mess.

Later, as I was flushing away still another mess, one of them decided to let loose one more time, and before I returned, Liam was proudly carrying a tasty bit of dog dropping around.

When I took them outside separately before lunch, things seemed back to normal. Rowan was first, which suited him just fine. Whenever he wanted to cut loose, he first glanced back at me to see whether I was ready to join him. Next came Molly, who liked to run zigzag in full flight. Other than that, she would go back to stillness, sitting and looking up at me, not moving until I petted her or picked her up. Liam, the last to go outside, would be doubtful and look at me as if to say, "No, that's all right, I'll stay in, thanks." Once outside, though, he'd run the length of the yard several times with me in hot pursuit before he settled down.

It was now mid-November, and all three discovered the joys of piles of leaves. They ran into them full tilt and crashed about, then flopped down and tried to bite every leaf. They didn't actually eat the leaves but just snapped at them and spit them to one side. I decided that they not only enjoyed crashing about in the leaves because of the sound, but that they were now able to make things fly every which way and I didn't seem to mind one bit.

From midafternoon on things cycled downward. First we took Rowan by himself into the living room with the business tray nearby. He used it frequently in the back kitchen, but in the living room he ignored the tray and wet on the floor. We showed him the error of his ways and cleaned up. Then he wet again on the papers and we praised him. Then he did a business in the tray and we gave him more praise. We brought Molly over, and within a few minutes Rowan wet again, this time on the rug. Again we showed him the error of his ways. After a while he wet again with only his front feet in the tray. Then, after Pat had to leave, he wet still again, this time on the rug. I returned him to the back kitchen, and when I was cleaning up his puddle, Molly wet on the rug, too. She also was returned to the back kitchen.

After I cleaned the rug I checked up on the three of them. The back kitchen floor was shiny with their wettings and their feet were wet from running through puddles. I cleaned them all up, put fresh paper down, and sat with them until they all were settled. By then it was time to leave them for supper. When I returned, they had strewn soggy papers all over the floor and were again wild. I cleaned up and again sat with them. They settled down briefly but then returned to destructive play until finally, about 9:30, they ran out of steam and collapsed. I took them upstairs and put all three in their den, telling them "No-o-o!" every time they half-heartedly tried to get out, and for once I had the bed all to myself. As the day had progressed I had again begun to feel ready to give up, to admit it was all a mistake being locked in with them for at least twenty hours a day, and to ask Leon to find them new owners. Fortunately, Pat had been appalled at the very idea.

2

Middle Puppyhood

Fifth Week

THIS NEXT step in their development marked a step forward for them as well as for us.

All three dogs, exhausted from their earlier wild behavior, were quiet for most of that first day of the new week. During the afternoon we took them outside for a subdued walk, and then before supper we had them join us in the living room for a try with the new plastic pan. Rowan did well the first time but then wet in the middle of the rug. We returned him to the back kitchen. Then Molly went to the pan and wet. We heaped extravagant praise upon her. We returned Rowan to the living room, and after a while he too wet in the pan, eliciting more praise. Then Liam wet in the pan to more whoops of delight. A little later Molly began investigating the floor, so I put her in the pan and she too wet again. After those two steps backward the previous week we were relieved to see a step forward and began to think that maybe there would be some hope after all.

The dogs continued to be on their best behavior at bedtime, and when it was time to turn out the light they were all curled up on the bed. Liam, as usual, had to go about 4:30, and I put the others down too, even though they wondered if that meant it was morning already. I assured them that no, it wasn't, and put the two big ones back on the bed. Liam decided that he wanted to curl up in the den, at least at first, but about an hour later he came over to the side of the bed. I reached over, found his center of gravity, and added him to the others.

The next day continued fairly well. After supper in the back kitchen they had a period of tussle and chase while I watched them from the rocker, and at one point, when they were a bit too wild, I started to get up just as Rowan thrust his foot under a runner. Amid much screeching Rowan leapt onto my lap. He first acted as though it was now the end of the road for him, but after I fussed over him for a few minutes, he pranced away ready to take on both the other dogs at once.

The next morning, November 20, I finished reading animal communicator Penelope Smith's book *Animal Talk*, and it added perspective to our relationship with the dogs. Earlier Pat had sat with all three for nearly an hour, and as usual after breakfast they began to spin out of control. After Pat left, I saw the stream of morning sunlight angling through the window onto the floor, remembered that I was supposed to be in retreat mode, and decided to try something different: I took each one up separately, held it in the sunlight, waited for the dog's attention, and said, "Do you like the sunlight? That's what you are, you know, a being of light." Another moment for attention, then, "We like your radiance, and we'd like you to be a companion. Can you do that?" Then I put each one down and sat on the floor by the sink. All three came over to me quietly. Molly curled up by my leg, and Liam climbed into my lap. Rowan hung around close by but seemed restless, pacing about, nudging the others, going into the den and biting its side. Finally I understood: he wanted to be Top Dog. I called him over, picked him up, and held him in my arms above the others, where he sagged contentedly into place.

During that day I followed the procedures from the Penelope Smith book—explaining things, talking to them as intelligent beings. It seemed to work. I had to leave them to give the outside windows their fall cleaning, but I explained it to them and told Rowan that he would have to be in charge. He listened carefully and promised to do the best he could. Pat took him for a walk outside so he could see me in action. After their lunch I let them play for a while and then hunkered down while they piled all over me. Later, when I sat in the rocker to read, the two big ones curled up by my feet and Liam wanted to be held.

When I left them to help Pat rearrange the living room, they did cut loose, and when I returned I took care of the wet papers they had tossed about and told them I was sorry I had left them so long, and then, one by one with their leashes, we took them on brief walks around the living room. Whenever I returned to the back kitchen, the ones still there would stop their cavorting and curl up by my feet.

After supper I dowsed which of them would be the one to take to the living room while we watched a movie, and Molly came out the highest. I explained the decision to Rowan and Liam and then went over with Molly, who curled up on my lap and dozed contentedly all through the movie. When I brought her back, I thanked the others (who had behaved themselves) for being so considerate.

They did take a small step backward later, running wildly about and not paying attention to discipline, but that night was the first time they went a full eight hours without a fuss. Their behavior seemed to verify the main point of the book, which was to offer a way to reach pets instead of just training them. Her approach seemed to be the next logical step for us to take.

For some time I had had a jokey correspondence with Pat's Uncle Jo, and when he learned that we had acquired three untrained puppies with winter nearly upon us, he called to say that he was interested to see how people's minds begin to go when they enter their sixties.

(11/20/94) I had suspected as much already, especially now, after a month of around-the-clock puppy duty. There have been

41

times—whole days—that have been a strain, but then a little voice says, hey, they've only been here on earth for three months, and they've still got a long, weedy period to go through, and besides, you dowsed that it was the thing to do to get them. How can I argue with that?

In the morning, after taking care of her plumbing, Molly now liked time to be able to go into the den all alone, bark at herself, and throw herself around. The guys didn't understand this at all, but Pat said she knew the feeling.

Liam was now dealing with an identity crisis. He was the one who most often barked (he had found his voice, and it was *yap-yap-yap*) and got the others going, and his eating was the most manic. We couldn't understand why he did it, so we asked him about it. He explained that he didn't like being the smallest and therefore number three. He figured that if he ate all he could from all three dishes, maybe he'd grow to be even bigger than Rowan. I had noticed that when he headed for another dish, it was usually Rowan's. He also figured that if he barked a lot, he could be even louder and more independent than Molly, and if he kept the others stirred up often enough, then he'd finally get to be Top Dog. We tried to tell him that he was just right the way he was, but we didn't think he was ready to accept that quite yet.

All three now liked times of being Special Dog. That morning it was Liam, and Pat took him over from the back kitchen to the main kitchen for his breakfast and afterward sat down with him so he could have all her attention. Later that day in the back kitchen, when all three started acting wild, I again lifted each one up for a talk. I told Rowan that he was a fine young male but as top dog he had to be good to the others, especially Molly. I reminded him about being a good companion. I told Molly that she didn't have to prove herself by egging the others on because we already knew that she was a fine figure of a female and that we valued her as a companion and wanted her to be her best self. I told Liam that he was really best when he tried to be himself and that he needed to help the others know how to behave. He didn't like that too well and walked away when I put him down, but after a few minutes of thinking things over, he came back and everything was okay. Again I sat on the floor, and again they piled all over me, companions to the core.

Near midday I started feeling queasy and light-headed, so I folded an old towel for my head and stretched out on the floor. That was new to the dogs, and they were quite excited. First they climbed all over me, and then Liam curled up on my stomach. Rowan stretched out beside me. Molly stood on my chest and stared down at me, finally deciding that it would be interesting to chew on my beard. I blew in her face, an action that astonished her. She studied the matter closely, so I blew in her face again, and she tried to pounce upon the source. By then I had started laughing, causing both her and Liam to bounce about, producing even more astonishment. When we finally sorted it all out, Molly and Rowan stretched out beside me while Liam took his chances on my stomach, and we all stayed that way for a good nap.

At one time during the afternoon I was away from the dogs for a while, and when I returned I hunkered down and greeted them all, telling them all how good they had been. Then Molly went to the middle of the floor, squatted, and wet. "Oh, Molly, no!" I said and cleaned up. Molly skulked around, then went to one side and lay down. After several minutes she arose, walked purposefully to the middle of the papers, squatted, and wet. I then praised her, the response she had been waiting for, and she came over to me, now all happy wiggles.

Because two of our friends were coming for dinner that evening, I had to spend quite a bit of time away from the dogs, and they did not respond well to being left alone. At first the two big ones tried to stretch out by the door, but Liam yapped them awake and soon they were all at it. The one who lost control the most was evidently Molly, who had the most persistent bark when overexcited. I went over to check on them several times. Within minutes while I was there they'd be quiet, but within minutes of my leaving they'd be wild. I had to remind myself yet again that they were only three months old.

Most of the days at the end of November proved stressful, either with dogs or with dog care added to other things. The company meal had gone all right, but it had required that Pat focus everything on that one event for most of the day and have me on deck for assistance, which meant that the dogs were left alone for long stretches. The next day, November 22, Doctor Susan was scheduled to arrive to give the dogs their second shots and then stay for supper. It was day 33, a significant retreat number, but Pat and I were tired and edgy and everything seemed to be out of balance. An added complication was that our friend Muriel had called about noon to see if it was all right to come over. I had told her that the vet was coming and would be staying for supper and that she was welcome to join us. Muriel arrived about 5:00, and we all went in with the dogs. About 5:40 Susan called to say that she had been held up with an emergency. She finally arrived about 7:00. Muriel didn't mind, because it gave her more time to be with "her" dog, Liam. Then came the official vet visit with brief examination and second shots. After that came the social time—appetizers, a large supper, and conversation, which continued until after eleven with pleasant, upbeat talk and a final round of holding the dogs and then watching them parade around on their leashes. It was midnight before everyone left and we were able to settle the dogs down for the night.

During the social part of the visit the dogs had one period of barking and paper playing, which I straightened out, and then when another such period began, this time with barking by Molly, I quieted them down, picked up Molly, and said, "No more barking!" She looked stubborn, so I added, "If you bark any more, you can't sleep with me tonight." She still looked stubborn, but she got the message. From then on there was no barking, to the amazement of Pat, Muriel, and Susan. I decided it would be better not to tell them what I had said to Molly. I had not, however, said anything to Molly about playing with wet papers, and later on, when I went in to check, I found that Molly had seen to it that a quantity of them had been quietly dragged into the den. I reprimanded her, but given the circumstances, I kept it mild.

Thanksgiving Day, the twenty-fourth, was tiring, and with the dogs spiraling into yet another period of restlessness and mulishness, there was little chance to do things that needed doing or to plan anything in advance. Liam had begun to change his manner of wetting, beginning on the paper and then walking off it and leaving behind a serpentine trail of dog pee. After I ate breakfast, showered, and dressed, they all wanted to be held on and off for the rest of the morning, creating a challenge in trying to read or use the computer with a dog on the lap, another held in one arm above the lap, and a third wrapped around a foot.

Our Thanksgiving dinner consisted of Cajun rice, cottage cheese, squash, cranberry jelly, and leftover cake. Ever since the dogs arrived, Pat had been fixing the equivalent of three from-scratch meals for them every day besides fixing meals for the two of us and for company, and since I had to stay with them, she had to do all the clean-up work plus everything else that needed doing. Her energy reserves were being stretched thin, but the only solution we knew of was simply to persevere, to remember that retreat focus and to continue to take one day at a time.

Sixth Week

By the beginning of their sixth week with us all three were becoming not only leggy but also assertively individual. Rowan barked for greeting and for protection, while Liam barked to say, "Notice me" or "Play with me." Molly barked when pursuing the other two. At night all three could now last seven or eight hours, but during the day they still wet every little while. They generally used the papers, but we still could not trust them alone in the main part of the house. Their play was still ruled by whoever wanted to keep it up, but if I picked up any one of them, that one would immediately become settled and when put back down would just wander around quietly.

Positive traits had now begun to surface more often. By Saturday morning, for instance, Rowan had lasted nine hours without having to get up, and then he waited until I had brought him downstairs to the back kitchen before he wandered over to the papers. I praised him and we tussled for a while before I went back to get the others. Likewise, however, negative traits remained strong. Rowan still experienced long periods of restlessness. Molly, like Liam, couldn't be left unsupervised because she'd still drag soggy papers all over the kitchen and into the den and then wet on the floor. When they played together, they were still apt to spin out of control and revert to their shrill, ear-piercing yaps.

In addition to the dog care and dog meals, Pat especially had to deal with late-November shop ads, finances, and customers, as well as the needs of friends and people who attended our center classes, the preparations for those classes, and various bodily pains and sleepless nights, all of which added to her wish to find a nice cave and be able to hibernate. Fortunately, those positive traits from the dogs continued to develop and brightened the dark periods. That Saturday each one, alone, was given the run of the living room. In turn they explored it, came when called, and showed a good, happy sense of play. When all three were there, they played "chase me" as fast as they could through the whole area. At various times all of them wanted to be held at once, even though there were only two laps available. We yearned for the time when they could have the freedom of the house without our having to watch them every second. I was feeling as exhausted as was Pat, and because the gloom of late November had set in, we again had dark moments of wondering what if anything was the meaning of it all.

During Saturday evening the dogs were out of control until I ignored my vows and slapped a rolled-up newspaper on the floor with a stern "No!" When I took them upstairs, they were immediately quiet and ready to be lifted onto the bed. Once there, they lay right down. Perhaps they suspected that if someone had called me on the telephone that very minute and asked, "Got any dogs for sale?" I would have said, "Yes, three."

That Sunday, the twenty-eighth, our center class went especially well, one of the most relaxed gatherings so far, and it helped to dispel some of the gloom. The dogs had started to be noisy, but after I talked with them, they were willing to remain quiet until the class was over, after which they were again full of lively, yappy play. When we took them over to the living room, they cut loose and began to forget about where to wet, so I drew them together and told them that the next time any one of them wet, they would all go back. Within two minutes Molly went to the center of the floor and wet, whereupon they all ended up in the back kitchen. I stayed with them until after they ate, and when I left to get a sandwich, they became wild. I tiptoed back and just stood in the doorway. Rowan saw me first and immediately stopped fooling around. Molly, her back to me, was still being wild, so Rowan gave her a meaningful glance. She looked around and also immediately stopped. I hadn't said a thing, but they knew that they had gone too far.

That afternoon I watched a Laurel and Hardy movie, *The Music Box*, and I understood the dogs a little better. They were acting a bit like The Boys after they delivered that piano, so when the poor owner arrived, I found myself viewing him with newfound sympathy. It was sort of like being with the dogs: day after day of Laurel and Hardy with me as the innocent bystander.

The next day I again felt that we had maybe three dogs too many. It wasn't that they were that awful, but their episodes of wildness were again affecting me really badly. By midmorning I felt a bit sick so again lay on the floor. At first they all piled over me, but then the two males wandered to their den and Molly was the only one who stayed curled up next to me. During the early afternoon, when they were wild, Pat came over and asked if I wanted to take a nap and I said no, I just wanted to get away from dogs for a while and to do something, anything, that didn't involve them. Fortunately they were growing tired, so for most of Pat's stay they snoozed. When I left, I had told Pat that for the time being I had little use for Rowan because he was so overbearing and arrogant to the others. He had evidently heard me, because when I returned the other two were curled up by the door and Rowan, usually the gregarious one, was all by himself in the den.

Later that afternoon we decided to take them to the living room for a run. I said to them, "The first one of you who wets can go to the living room," and Liam immediately went to the paper and wet. After letting Liam enjoy being Only Dog, I returned to the back kitchen and Rowan made a point of going to the paper and wetting as soon as I walked in, so he was next. Then came Molly, who had wet on her own in her own good time when I wasn't around.

3

Late Puppyhood

BY NOW Rowan was the one most clearly going through growing pains and losing it with both plumbing and sense of companionship. Liam was now the first one to know when I had really had it. He was also way ahead of Rowan in learning to wet with one leg raised, although at that point all he could manage was a drunken swagger from one leg to the other. Molly was becoming the one most aware of me and wanting, in her quiet way, to be noticed or held, even though Pat noted that she was still a terribly irksome pest with the others.

On the last day of November I noted another slight difference in their behavior. Rowan acted less aggressive toward the others. Molly said, "Hold me" much of the time, which meant whenever I tried to read or go hither and yon, Molly would be draped over my arm. Liam now yapped less often. During the evening in the living room, they enjoyed a three-way tussle until it began to develop into a real dogfight. After I sorted it out, they again realized that they had gone too far, and they became very quiet, practically tiptoeing around each other until bedtime.

The next day, December 1, I noted that over the course of two weeks Liam had gained another pound in chubbiness and had finally begun to sort out his identity crisis. He barked less often, although each yap still sliced through the eardrums. Molly had become quite feminine and took it for granted that I would hold her whenever she so desired. That day was mostly wrapping day for gifts that needed to be mailed. The dogs would begin to go wild at my absence, but every time I tiptoed back and stood in the doorway, they immediately stopped and became extra calm, and when I picked up papers and straightened up the room, they milled about as though thinking, "Oh darn, we did it again." At mealtimes they now knew that they were fed in a certain order. First Rowan got his dish, then Molly, and then Liam. They were learning to wait their turns by standing in the places where their food would be put down.

Seventh Week

The worst of the earlier stress was passing, and Pat reminded me that the time with the dogs should be viewed as retreat time and that everything I noted about the dogs should relate to some process I should notice about myself. I wasn't clear how peeing on the rug fit in, except that maybe it meant that in time I too would cease my wild behavior and uncontrolled barking.

That night we all slept soundly for eight hours, making it clear that Pat knew what she was talking about.

On Saturday the third Pat went to a craft show in St. Johnsbury, so I was alone with the pack for a day. In the morning they played, gnawed at the rocker, and napped. Around noon they cleared themselves out and had lunch. During the afternoon they milled about. After Pat returned around 4:00 we took them into the living room, but Molly was the only one who settled down next to me on the couch. Rowan ran about, then forgot and wet on the rug. Liam quivered restlessly until I returned him to the back room, where he immediately wet and did business. It was still the time of the doldrums, but in a nice way, for both the dogs and their keepers.

By Sunday those doldrums were over but not in a nice way, and it ended up one of the worst days so far if not the worst.

All three were as bad as possible, and by late afternoon I was really, really ready to be rid of them, even to give them away if anyone happened to stop by. It didn't help, either, that I had come down with a difficult headache and that the seasonal stress of wrapping and packaging Christmas presents had reached its peak. The dogs evidently had been picking up on the stress, because they tried to match it in the only ways they knew. When I tried to consolidate the dog papers and wetting box in one corner, all three revolted and refused to use that area. When they indicated that they had to go, I put them in that area, and they immediately left it and wet all over the floor. At one point Liam had to wet, ran toward the wetting box, and at the last moment stepped back to the middle of the floor. I had to do outside work, too, and in the time I was gone all three again did businesses everywhere and turned the floor into a lake.

That evening, when I was preparing the room and bed, I leaned over just so and my back went *whunk!* For a few minutes I collapsed onto the bed until the pain eased a bit, then made the effort to stand up, and very carefully finished preparing the bed while holding my body in odd positions. All that may have contributed to why I felt that for whatever reasons, it was six weeks down the drain and that nothing positive was happening after all. I thought that maybe it wouldn't be such a bad idea to give up on the retreat idea, put an advertisement in the paper, sell the shelties, and then try again with a collie.

We had thought that the experiences Sunday were as bad as they could get, and then came Monday. During the night my back went *twang* every time I moved, and getting out of bed to tend to the dogs was an engineering feat. In addition, my headache worsened, and by 5:30 it was a bad as it was possible for a headache to get. By midmorning I couldn't even keep four drops of Rescue Remedy down and had to use Compazine to stop the retching. The migraine then went from as bad as could be to even worse until midafternoon, and it wasn't until suppertime that it started to lift enough that I could keep down rice and bouillon. All of that meant that Pat literally had to do everything in a day already heavily scheduled, and the dogs did everything they could do to test her.

By the next day I felt much better, and all three dogs returned to being well behaved and responsive. Pat had another heavily scheduled day with things outside the home in the morning and deskwork waiting for her in the afternoon. In spite of the better behavior of the dogs, it was the feeling of being trapped that made everything seem difficult. The dogs had obviously been feeling trapped, too, and all four of us knew it was time to sit, breathe, and refocus. A time out period helped us feel better, and we decided to keep going a while longer.

All three beasties were now at the peak leggy and chunky stage. Molly was entering her inelegant adolescence, Rowan was beginning to show that he might just possibly be able to become a responsible young dog, and Liam, the butterball, was still trying to find himself. I made them a new toy, a block of hardwood with an old sock wrapped around it. My theory was that it would keep them from chewing the floor of their den. It did for a while, too, except that once they stopped being suspicious of it, they all wanted to claim it at the same time, which meant that I had to find two more blocks of hardwood and two more old socks. That worked for a while, but then Liam decided that he could continue to find himself more easily if he claimed possession of all three socks.

Tuesday evening we began decorating the living room, and we brought the dogs over one by one. Rowan showed great interest in everything we did. I returned him when something told me it was time to do so, and he immediately wet. When Molly came over, she ran about and investigated behind everything she could get behind. Liam seemed over-joyed at being able to run around but also a bit overwhelmed. Everything seemed different to him. He didn't know what to do when I called him or approached him, and he suspect-ed the worst. None of them, though, did any wetting in the room, which was a relief.

All three were back to being alert and interested, and when-ever I appeared they again tumbled about and wiggled their greetings. If I headed into the laundry alcove off the back kitchen, they furiously tried to follow me in, and when the clanking of the machines began, they were sure that some-thing awful was happening to me and that they should come to my rescue. When I reappeared, they sported about in re-lief. Whenever I put anything new on the floor, they circled it and worried at it until they could figure out what it was. If I even stood or sat in a different spot than usual, they would all come over to see what was going on. So I decided that maybe there was still hope for all of us and maybe I wouldn't need to put an ad in the paper after all.

Wednesday was the day all three wanted total attention and exclusive rights to be held, which meant that I was one-third successful at any one time. After lunch Pat and I made the front room, main kitchen, and living room dog-proof and went over every corner with the vacuum cleaner. Then we brought the dogs over and tried to explain to them that if they were orderly and quiet they could stay. They weren't, so back they went.

That evening I let them play around a bit in my study, and when they drifted toward the bed, I lifted them onto it. They grudgingly gave me room to join them, and soon Liam ad-opted his Piglet position: on his back, legs every which way, head back. The other two continued to sleep like, well, dogs.

The next morning, when I lifted them off the bed to go downstairs, my back went *whunk* again, so dressing and carrying them downstairs ended up being another engineering feat.

After breakfast Pat had to go out for a while, and when she returned she took Rowan over to her work area in the front room. This was a first for him, and he whooped around with much barking until he finally just snooped and explored. Then he had still another brand-new experience. Pat put him into a little sweater, and we both took him in the car up to the post office. He whimpered most of the way up and back while Pat held him, but once he was safely back at the house, he realized that he had really and truly had an adventure, and he told the other two all about it in some detail.

The most difficult thing with Liam was still that he was so small. He had also become so solidly chubby that it was difficult to get hold of him, and whenever I picked him up and arranged him in my arms, he made weird little grunts, making it difficult to take him seriously as a dog.

Thus ended the seventh week, the one during which things had totally hit bottom, followed by our again being ready to give up, but then having glimpses that there was still hope for the dogs as well as for their clueless owners.

Eighth Week

Friday, December 9, marked their fiftieth day with us. Liam now walked with greater self-possession, Molly carried herself with increased delicacy, and Rowan, solid of body, was attaining a greater air of responsibility, but even so, all three still largely showed the same swirl of generic dogginess. As they grew into their world and ours, they had to accommodate themselves to both. One of our jobs was to help direct them, just as one of their jobs was to show their willingness to be directed.

During the day little things and extraneous duties kept cropping up, and main plans kept being put off and then put off some more. The dogs couldn't find a rhythm to their activity-rest cycle because just as rest time began for all of us, along would come a visitor or a customer to the shop, providing them with reason to want to remain alert and noisy.

Molly, now the one most restless, wanted either to egg on the others or to charge about on her own. She again had little interest in being held, and when I took her into the living room before lunch, she refused to come when called. She didn't run hither and yon around the room either, preferring to snoop about. After I attended to customers in the shop and chatted with friends who stopped by, I noted that the back kitchen had a different odor. It wasn't one of wet papers or hidden droppings, although it seemed associated with them. I noticed it most strongly when I picked Molly up and smelled her fur, which meant that even though she wouldn't be in heat for another four months, she did seem to be going through some sort of hormonal change.

The guys continued to be guys, although Liam was now more sensitive than ever. That morning I caught him just starting to drag a sheet of paper and said "Liam! No!" a bit too sharply. He dropped it and crept away, back hunched, tail between his legs, walking as though all four feet hurt, and occasionally looking back at me with a beaten look. I picked him up and tried to reassure him that it was really all right and that he was a very nice and very special dog even though he mustn't drag papers around. It took a while to convince him.

The next morning, Saturday, Liam curled up on my lap, perfectly willing to be Tiny Dog for a while after an early morning session of egging the others onward and being egged on in return. He still didn't understand that it made little difference how much he ate, that he would not grow beyond his normal little-guy size. He couldn't comprehend that he should take in only as much as his system needed and that most of what he ate went in one end and out the other anyhow, with only the needed stuff left behind, and then anything else would end up as pudginess so that instead of growing larger, he'd feel uncomfortable and grunt while his system tried to handle the overload. At the same time Rowan, who ate the same amount as he did, grew even larger and more muscular all the time. Liam found it all very discouraging.

I began to see that whole situation as similar to how people relate to spiritual activities. They decide that if they read more material or go to more retreats or do more practices, they will become even more "spiritual." They don't understand that they can take in only what can be assimilated at the time, and just as with Liam, the excess would probably end up going in one end and out the other and they too would end up very discouraged. Perhaps there is a kind of spiritual DNA that determines the final "size" of one's spiritual self in its earthly form, and that size is the one that is appropriate.

For the rest of the day the dogs were surprisingly good, with only subdued milling and tussling. I had put a little folded blanket under my desk, and they had all tried it out. If they started to tussle there or chew it, I told them they couldn't because it was a sanctuary area. So far they had listened. And by late afternoon, when they ran out of steam, they all curled up on the blanket while I prepared for the next day's center class.

Sunday started well after a quiet night. They slept for eight solid hours, did routine businesses, ate good breakfasts, and behaved themselves well until yet another class was over and everyone had left. We had started our study of Attar's *The Conference of the Birds* and went over the difficulties the well-meaning flock undergoes on their quest to reach the Simurgh—only to discover at the end that they were the Simurgh they had been seeking and that their entire outward quest had ended up being a quest within. The class related to it well.

During late afternoon and evening the dogs were full of energy that stayed on the edge of spinning out of control.

Whenever I was away and Liam or Molly began frenzied barking, I knew that paper was being dragged about and torn into small pieces. I'd try to remain as quiet as I could as I returned. When they did hear me approaching, they were all ready to greet me, and they would look at the paper as though they hadn't any idea at all about how in the world it got there. Whenever I caught them in the act, they stopped and made believe they were really heading somewhere else. If I spoke to one who still had paper in its mouth, that one would let go of it without missing a beat and deny any connection with it. They were no longer feeling terribly guilty about messing with the paper; they just never did it when I was around.

By evening the restless one was Molly. She continually picked on the two males, and when they finally curled up on the blanket under the desk, she continued to roam around, at one point digging frenziedly at the linoleum. Finally, after pacing around some more, doing a business, and checking the room for a last time, she too stretched out on the blanket.

The next day, Tuesday, our Canadian friend Bob stopped by to see if any packages had arrived for him. He usually stopped by once a week, and each time he saw the dogs, he said, "They've grown." I didn't particularly notice it, but the comment helped to explain why they did seem to take up a bit more space on the bed. And on Monday Rowan had discovered that he was able to reach up and put his front paws on my desk—no mean feat for a sheltie. Actually he put his feet on the computer keyboard and accessed strange commands and symbols I didn't even know were there. In the living room he could now jump off and on the couch with ease, and he was just starting to be able to climb stairs. Whenever I now held him, he took up my whole lap. From time to time I told him that he was especially valued as a footman, which I guess he understood, because whenever he curled up on the floor, it was usually on one of my feet.

I hadn't noticed Molly's growing, except that whenever I weighed her, she was always a quarter pound or half pound heavier. I did notice that her coat was becoming a bit fuller, that she had more mood swings, and that she was developing an increased sense of Mollyness. So I didn't think, Oh, she's grown. Any changes were simply because she was Molly, not because she was getting larger. On Wednesday I took a short nap, and she had the honor of joining me. She had decided that it was nice being away from the others and alone with me for a while, and we both had a good snooze.

Later that day Doctor Susan came by briefly to give them their third shots, but she had to return to the clinic for an appointment rather than stay for supper. She was greeted by much barking, partly protective and partly sheer bluster, which Rowan had trouble shutting off. None of them were comfortable with her this time, even though she tried to be as friendly as possible. Her first comment, though, was, "They look like they're all on stilts!" So I was right; they were all going through a gawky, leggy period.

Liam was the first to be looked over, and he was not happy about it. In fact, he wanted none of it at all. He fought having his heartbeat checked, his ears checked, and his teeth looked at. He was almost too wild to hold, and he even wet his pants for the first time ever. Then I had to hold him really securely on the table so that he could receive his shot, and afterward he went to the far corner of the den, drew into himself, and looked abused. Rowan, still full of bluster, was also very uneasy about being looked over but put up only token resistance. Molly took it all as a matter of course, allowing all sorts of looking over as long as I was holding her. The needle seemed to sting her more than it did the others, but all she did was tighten up. After Susan left I thought they would all want a nap, but the experience had made them ready for a play spell. We took our chances and left them to their own devices, one of which was to drag papers all over.

I stayed with them while they had their supper, and then Pat and I enjoyed having the living room all to ourselves. Earlier I had vacuumed, picked up, and built a good fire in the woodstove because we had thought that Susan would be staying. So we had about an hour of eating a fancier than usual meal and sitting in a freshly cleaned room without dogs.

It was then, though, that Liam had problems. I went over to check on them, and Liam whimpered every time Rowan sniffed or pawed him. I tried to pick him up, and it hurt him so much that he squealed. At first Pat thought I was coddling him a bit too much, but when she tried to hold him, he yipped and whimpered steadily. Afterward we thought it was some sort of internal bloat from something he ate or maybe an aftereffect of the fear he had shown with Susan. First I lay on the bed with him, and then at bedtime Pat looked after the other two while I carried Liam downstairs, made him comfortable, and cleaned up the back kitchen. I then took him back up to my study and placed him on his special spot near the top of the bed and told the others to stay near the foot, which they did without any great urging. They realized that Liam felt poorly and that I was serious.

That evening did give us pause about all three dogs, and Pat said that the experience made her aware that Liam was now no longer "Muriel's dog" but one of our dogs.

That night Liam whimpered about 2:00, so I put him down and he did everything. Pat got up, too, just in case he was worse. While we were checking Liam, the other two rearranged themselves in the warm center of the bed. I had to move them to get back in, and all three curled up together. By morning Liam was better, so that when I took them downstairs they were ready for active play with Liam ready to make up for lost time.

I noted on Wednesday that Molly, although gawky, was now trying out various shades of provocative behavior, especially on Rowan. She would make a pest of herself sniffing and biting him at random, then sinking her teeth in and try-ing to drag him. When he responded, they'd tussle and chase for a while, and when he tried to nap, she'd be at him again. Then she would suddenly decide she had had enough and come running to me with her "save me" attitude, wanting to be picked up and fussed with while Rowan roamed about, much like any other bewildered male.

Rowan joined me for my nap that day. At first he decided he was in no mood for a nap and couldn't settle down. Finally he sort of lay down, and soon he snoozed comfortably. Later, when it was time to go back downstairs, he stretched out in all directions, evidently enjoying the unlimited space avail-able to one dog alone on the bed.

I had been reading *The Art of Raising a Puppy* by the Monks of New Skete, and all their information related to having one puppy. One. Based on what they said, I decided that by now any one of our three by itself would have become a well-trained paragon. Three puppies, we had discovered, were nine times as difficult to raise as one puppy, and my suspicion, later confirmed, was that it would take nine times as long before they would be trained to the house.

The next morning marked the beginning of the last day of their first eight weeks with us. I weighed all three and found that they had all doubled in weight, with Rowan adding an extra pound. Their bodies had become more solid, so I guessed that their next growth spurt would be in the body rather than in the legs. That next growth spurt evidently kicked in that very day, because they attacked all three meals with such frenzy that we had to move Liam to another room.

During the afternoon things in general began to unravel, but it wasn't really the fault of the dogs. Shortly after 1:00 Pat arrived home with food items to fit into the freezer and refrigerator. I left the dogs long enough to help her unload and sort things out, during which time Liam did a huge wet in the middle of the floor. I covered it up and expressed my disappointment. Then a customer arrived, one of those inter-minable lookers who tell you what a nice shop you have but who don't buy anything, so it wasn't until 3:00 that the dogs finally got their lunch, by which time they were in a state and went into another feeding frenzy, with Molly and Rowan so vicious that I had to grab them both by the scruff of the neck and force them apart. I picked up their dishes before Pat re-turned with Liam, and even then, with no food in sight, they ran about wildly and growled at each other for quite a while.

It wasn't until late afternoon that they tried to make up for their behavior. I left them alone for half an hour while I tend-ed the fire in the woodstove and watched the news, and when I returned, everything in the back kitchen was still orderly. I took that as a sign.

The meals had been delayed that day in part because Pat had been giving them a homeopathic remedy to offset ill effects from their last shots, and they had to wait an hour before being fed. That morning they didn't get their remedy until about 7:15, and because Pat then had to go out, they didn't eat breakfast until about 8:45. Later she had to go gro-cery shopping, so it was 3:00 before things were sorted out and unloaded and lunch was prepared, which made the mid-day meal very late. That evening it was after 8:30 before they could have their suppers. Each meal was still a special one made from scratch, which meant that for the most part the dogs were eating better, more nutritious meals than we were.

At bedtime, which ended up being only about half an hour after they ate, the dogs couldn't quite figure out what time it really was, but after a brief period of milling about, they settled down and slept until 7:15 except, of course, for Liam, who as usual had to wet during the night.

So at the end of the eighth week the puppies were still in the middle of things rather than being nicely matured, and although those things were now flowing toward harmony, they hadn't arrived there yet. They had now been with us for exactly half their lives, and in a couple of days they would be officially four months old.

Ninth Week

During that Friday afternoon I took Rowan outside on his leash. He had never been in snow, and at first he didn't much notice it. We trotted to the backyard, he sniffed about, and we trotted back to where the plow had cleared our driveway. We explored that area and then, when I tried to get him to go for another trot to the backyard, he dug in his heels. He had discovered that snow was cold, especially on tender little paws, and he wanted no more of it. Although we stayed out while he paced the plowed area, he balked at the idea of venturing out again into the deeper snow.

We took all three over to the living room but kept them on their leashes, partly because we had a good fire in the woodstove and Pat worried that one of them might rub against the stove. When we returned them to the back kitchen, Molly headed right for the paper to wet and Rowan wet in the tray with the paper. Liam was not concerned at all about paper and just let loose as he staggered around the room and left another one of those complicated trails. When I tapped the floor and said "Oh, no!" he crept into the den and sat very worried in one of its corners.

They continued to enjoy their toys—the socks and the pieces of wood—but they seemed to like it better if I first made a deal of it by playing "sock" or "wood" with them. It reminded them that yes, those things were toys. Naturally they would all go after the same one at the same time, which meant that there were occasional quarrels. Whenever that happened, I'd simply wave around another one and immediately that one became the only one worth pursuing. If the other two became distracted, Liam carried all the toys into the den. If a game of "sock" became a tug of war between Liam and one of the others, he was at a disadvantage because they could drag him all over the floor. He discovered, though, that if he tugged from inside the den, the other dog would have to drag the whole box around.

The next day was a good day, and even though we had a friend stop by for a visit and lunch, the dogs made no plumbing mistakes and dragged no papers. Later, when I was with them and they were at loose ends, we all played "follow," which meant that I walked around the room in a silly way and they all followed me. If I turned sharply, they had to do the same. They all thought it was great fun, but I was just as glad that no one was watching.

The eighteenth was clean-up day, and except for their barking all three continued their good behavior. When I left them to make fresh coffee they began a great round of noise, and when I returned I said, "Molly, was that you barking?" She replied, "Yes! Yes! Yes!" Puppyhood was drawing to a close.

4

Early Adolescence

Late December

DURING THE last two weeks of the year, the curtain began to close on puppyhood. The dogs appeared to walk around on stilts. Rowan and Liam grew more restless, and Molly became even more contrary, pestering me to pick her up, but once up, pestering me to put her down. Liam acted belligerent toward the others, and Rowan outdid Molly with his barking. Molly developed the largest and softest ruff, and although Rowan was developing the thickest coat, that soft ruff made Molly's more noticeable. They still made plumbing mistakes, but by now they were less frequent.

Although we noted steps forward during daytime, the steps backward often began at bedtime. When I turned the lights out they'd now be ready for a wild time in the dark, and once downstairs in the morning they'd again be wild, so much so that I moved their den to one side so they wouldn't demolish it. They had found it was exciting to go to one end of the room, run full tilt into the den, and stop by smashing into one of the inside walls, after which they'd go seemingly berserk, rolling about in the confined space and trying to destroy each other.

On the morning of December 19, following their wild time, I prepared myself a quick breakfast, a bowl of cold, gelatinous oatmeal—in reality leftover dog food. I could have warmed it up, but then it would have become warm, gelatinous leftover dog food. Even though it was gooey, I hoped that it would give me the energy it seemed to give the dogs every morning. If it did, it meant that at any moment I too would go crashing around the floor, tossing old socks every which way. The urge to do so did arise, but I managed to keep it in check.

By midafternoon their wild behavior began to smooth out, and when Pat went out for two hours I was able to do dishes, start a fire in the woodstove, and generally clean up. Customers came to the shop and actually spent money. By bedtime all three puppies settled right down on the bed, even choosing spots that allowed me to settle down too.

That evening Pat commented that she thought the dogs now really wanted to please. I hadn't particularly noted it myself, except that they were more conscientious about using papers and each one now showed more desire to be Only Dog. They had roiled about after supper but stopped when I said "No-o-o!" Pat reminded me that we were just getting over three key days of the full moon, which may have explained why I had decided to start the day with cold, gelatinous leftover dog food and thought about tossing socks about. In any event, earlier that day I made a curious observation. Liam had been off by himself in the den, and when I looked at him, it was as though someone else was looking at me through Liam's eyes. I tried to dowse what was going on and came up with an intriguing response: Liam was now being invested with new spirit—not an interloper but his real self. Up to then Liam had been sort of the unformed little guy, and I felt that this change might be Liam's version of the hormonal change Molly experienced a week earlier. Something had triggered that new spirit into life, and I looked forward to seeing how it would affect Liam's behavior and physical being.

The next afternoon, because Liam still yapped whenever anyone entered the shop, I had to pick him up and hold him while he kept a close eye on any customers, who would usually comment that he was the most adorable thing they had ever seen. During the evening I brought him over while we watched part of a movie, and after a few restless minutes he stretched out on the couch. I brought Molly over too, but she both wanted and didn't want to be there. I ended up standing and holding her for the remainder of the show.

Molly and Rowan had now grown coats that could be combed, and they decided that being combed was another game even though they weren't clear about its rules. They still followed me when I walked around the room, and if I took off one of my shoes, they attacked my sock and tried to subdue it while my toes wiggled in stark defiance. And whenever I put a new object on the floor, they circled it and sniffed carefully, sometimes giving it a good barking, just in case.

That night Liam continued to be betwixt and between. About midnight he whimpered that he wanted to be put down. I carried him over to the paper, and he stood there and did nothing. Then he walked to the middle of the room and sat down. I stood him on the paper again, but all he did was assume his "beaten" posture, so I went back to bed while he sat near the paper and just looked at me. I went to sleep, but I think that shortly after that he went into the den for several hours and sort of hung around. Then he made a noise, a mix of groan and sigh, and came near the bed. I reached down and put him back on it, after which he curled up with the others and slept. He apparently had decided simply to try out his independence for a while, because the papers were still pristine in the morning.

Wednesday marked the first day of winter even though the temperature had risen to fifty degrees, making it too slushy to take dogs out. Before supper we did bring them over to the living room, again one at a time. Rowan stayed for a while but couldn't settle down. Liam curled up nicely, first in my lap and then in Pat's. Molly didn't want to be held, didn't particularly want to come when called, and simply wandered about.

That morning I had put the central tube from some wrapping paper onto the floor. First they circled it warily, then they barked at it wildly, and then they retreated, Molly to my lap and the others to their den. I had no idea what they thought it was. Pat told me that they did the same thing earlier when she put it on the floor. I had been taking a nap at the time, and I had sort of wondered what all the barking was about.

Thursday, the end of their ninth week here, was a day of highs and lows. In the morning the dogs cooperated fully, and since it was less slushy, Rowan had a good walk, after which I wrapped Pat's Christmas gifts and then lay on the floor for a doze. All three climbed all over me, not knowing whether it was time for a game or whether it was bedtime or whether it was all over for me. I think they decided it might be a combination of all three, so they stayed close.

By midday things took a downturn. While Pat was preparing their lunch, the water-filtering system broke. Feeling frustrated and pressured, I unearthed an older water filter, cleaned it out, and set it up, during which time the dogs tuned in to my feelings and all did businesses, dragging them all over the floor and into their den, and messing up wet papers so that I had to reclean the floor and wash all their bedding. Pat then went upstairs to take a nap while I prepared for the evening center class to be held in the living room. The group found it pleasant to be there instead of in the front room of the shop, especially with the tree lights on, but the ambience was totally different, since we were spread out instead of sitting around a smallish table. It seemed a challenge to get through the class, but I must have been relaxed about it because the dogs behaved so well in the back kitchen that Pat was able to join us for a healing circle.

The remainder of the month was a time of either frustration or winter doldrums. Every morning the dogs continued with their periods of wild behavior. When I took all three outside on the twenty-third, though, they did enjoy romping about in the snow, and Molly felt that she could have stayed outside all day. During their mealtimes we still had to feed Liam in another room, and I had to hold Molly and Rowan by their ruffs so that they wouldn't start a food fight.

In general during that time the dogs remained relatively quiet if I stayed with them, often curling up at my feet. If I were to remove my footwear, though, they'd leap to their favorite game and attack my stockinged foot to subdue the wiggling creature within. In the living room Liam was the one who now preferred to curl up between us while the other two snooped about restlessly, and he was beginning to show that he really wanted to hold it in during the night. Sometimes he'd make little grunts while on the bed. I'd put him down, sometimes up to three times during the night, and he'd simply stand around until I lifted him back onto the bed. I decided it was all because that new self was sorting itself out with the old self.

About this time Molly discovered that she could shut the door to the back kitchen. Whenever I wasn't around, she gave it enough of a push that it would close and click shut. On Christmas morning Pat and I sat by the tree in the living room for a while with our coffee, and although Molly had closed the kitchen door, the dogs behaved so well that I chose to overlook the remains of bits of business scattered around the floor and in their den.

We tried bringing them to the living room one at a time as we opened presents, but each one became wild and had to be returned. Then we tried all three at the same time, but their wildness continued. Finally I had to return Molly to the back kitchen, and while I was gone Rowan did a huge wet on the rug right next to the wetting bin that was lined with paper. He went back, too, while Pat held Liam and reassured him that no, he wasn't the one being scolded and could remain with us. At lunchtime, while Pat and I listened to music, Molly again shut the door and all three rampaged. When

I later cleaned everything up and put down fresh paper, they seemed relieved. They liked to toss things about, but they no longer liked a messy room.

One of my Christmas presents from Pat was a book on Shetland sheepdogs. I noted that all the pictures in the book were either of tiny puppies or mature dogs, with no pictures of shelties in the leggy, ungainly, practically hairless early adolescent stage that the three beasties were now in, the stage that Eugene called the stage of the uglies. Muriel's present to the dogs was a chain that allowed two of them to be led from one leash. We tried it outside with Molly and Liam, and although they enjoyed cavorting in the snow, they couldn't quite work out how to coordinate their speed and direction.

Wednesday we had to prepare for a huge potluck gathering of friends and center people to be held at our house the next day. We knew from experience that some of the guests would bring small dishes of things better left untouched, so Pat made two cakes, one sage bread, various vegetable dishes, a large salad, punch, and an even larger vegetarian casserole. My main focus was to try to repair a computer error. The machine had frozen up and the floppy disc had gone all funny. After a daylong effort of recovery, I retrieved a small percentage of material from the disc and decided that dogs and their owners weren't the only things that sometimes went all funny. That evening I was able to help Pat with the last of the cakes, and after feeding the dogs their supper and giving them a brief run of the house, we again collapsed into bed, where all five of us more or less slept until 6:30, awakening only when the wind caused the house to creak or when a snowplow alerted the dogs to protective mode.

The gathering the next day went well, but it was fortunate that Pat had prepared as she did because hardly anybody brought anything edible. The dogs acquitted themselves well, too. At first they put up a great storm whenever anyone arrived, but later, when I brought them over to the group one at a time, they were in timid mode. Whenever I held Rowan close to anyone, he first barked with great bluster and then tried to escape. Molly tried to remain casual, but she shook. Liam both shook and squirmed to be let go even though, as always, everyone thought he was the most darling thing they had ever seen. Then, after all three were carried back to the kitchen, their next trip over went surprisingly well, and Rowan was even willing to be led around by his leash. Our vet, Susan, was one of the guests, and she thought Liam was a bit chunkier than he should be and suggested cutting back on his food just a bit. I wasn't sure whether Liam agreed with her or not.

That morning, after assisting in the kitchen and showering, I had dressed in clothes and shoes that the dogs had never seen. When I appeared in the back kitchen, they fell about in turmoil with great wiggling, running about, and bashing against me. Anything new excited them, and suddenly there I was, all new.

The morning after the potluck all three were bursting with energy. Pat accused Molly of being a holy terror when left to her own devices and then, whenever I picked her up, of putting on an act of becoming Molly Meek. Liam showed his energy by becoming super bossy, demanding to be picked up or catered to. Rowan enjoyed engaging in playful attacks at the other dogs and at me. It all seemed an improvement over their going berserk.

Rowan's ruff began to come out in odd ways so that he looked unkempt even after I combed him. Two odd looking tufts of thick, light hair were also coming out on either side of his tail, making him look vaguely jet propelled. Pat said that she had noticed similar tail fins on Molly. There weren't any on Liam, but he was still busy finding himself.

Later that day Liam briefly took a step backward. I had to leave them for a few minutes, and I returned to find the remains of droppings on the paper and a very guilty looking Liam. We were, however, again experiencing the three strongest days of the new moon, so I simply cleaned it all up without a word.

During the last day of the month the new moon continued to have its effect. The dogs started the day in good humor and friendly play but then, as the day progressed, it was as if they had never received any training at all, which meant another day of cleanup, and in the living room Molly went into stupid mode and Liam became a brainless puppy. Rowan contented himself with dribbling about in long streams across the rug. And so the year drew to a close.

January

During the first week of the new year Molly finally subdued those cardboard tubes. Rowan was still cautious, and Liam acted bored, but Molly circled the tubes, lunged toward them, scrabbled at them with her forepaws, and finally gave them a bash. Then she leaped away, circled them some more, and bashed them anew. Every now and then I picked one up, pointed it at her, and make a rude sound through it, after which she'd have to subdue it all over again.

On the morning of the third I took Rowan and Liam downstairs first, and Molly was very put out to be left. After I started a pot of coffee and returned, she made a point of taking little notice of me—not coming when called, not responding to being petted. She just sat and looked crushed. I took her down with the others, left to get coffee, and by the time I returned she had decided to forgive me and let me hold her.

Twice during the day I played "cardboard tube" with all three of them, rude sounds and all, and this time they all joined in and whooped it up. When mealtime approached, though, they stopped and looked toward the other kitchen three rooms away on the other side of the house. When their plates finally arrived they went into a newly discovered jumping-jack routine, popping up and down several times almost to their own height. Their ferocious behavior was over, and when I put Rowan's dish down, Molly made no attempt to head for it, waiting patiently until I put hers down a little distance away.

I also began a training session in the living room with Rowan, first walking him about on his leash, which he liked, and having him come on command, which he also liked. He sat when directed to do so, maybe because he knew it meant that he would be praised and stroked. We then had a silly play spell followed by a snooze while I held him. Later I took the others over for the same training. Liam cooperated fairly well, and Molly reluctantly cooperated, which rather surprised and pleased me.

All three now received a combing every day. Rowan took to it best, while Molly and Liam both understood it to be a game even though they still couldn't figure out the precise rules.

The next day, the fourth, was mixed, partly because Pat wasn't sure whether she should go into town or not. She finally decided to tend to other things locally while I finished the book on the art of raising a puppy and learned about all the things I had been doing wrong for weeks and weeks. It was just as well that Pat decided not to go into town, because the following day, when I tried to start the car to go to the post office, the battery died. Benny, our garage man, came up and said that it was shot and had to be replaced. If Pat had gone into town, it might well have died in the Grand Union parking lot.

That evening Pat retired early while I returned to the back kitchen and finished some work for the next day's center class with all three dogs curled up at my feet.

Because of somewhat dicey weather, only three people showed up for that class, so we all moved in close around the warm wood stove and mostly chatted about various retreat experiences, which made a rather nice ending to a day that had involved getting the car to the garage and then picking it up hours later in bad weather.

Before the center class began, all three attendees admired the dogs and commented on how much they had grown. Not only that but their manes were getting larger, too—Molly's nicely and neatly, Rowan's in scruffy bunches, and Liam's just barely, even though he was making good progress with those tail feathers.

The sixth day came and went rapidly. Pat did grocery shopping in town, followed by dog lunches and a much-needed nap. The dogs followed suit, and suddenly it was time for supper and dog training, following which, to our surprise, all three draped themselves around us on the living room couch and snoozed. Afterward I returned them to the back kitchen for a round of wetting and then carted them upstairs and lifted them onto the bed. They were restless but cooperative, and Rowan enjoyed a few meditative chews on the edge of a blanket.

Pat's observation regarding Molly remained accurate: whenever I picked her up, she was cuddlesome, and when I put her back down, she was a pest and bedeviled the other two by outstaring them, playfully mouthing their ruffs and then suddenly biting, and generally annoying them when they were trying to rest. She wasn't going into heat, but she certainly seemed to be getting in practice to do so.

The seventh day, like the previous one, seemed to be over in no time. In the morning I shoveled outside and prepared for yet another center class, and during the day the dog cycle was play, sleep, play, sleep. Then supper. Then living-room training. Then bed.

Day number eight marked the last day of a second period of forty days and forty nights—significant numbers for an extended retreat—as well as the first day of a week with strong ups and downs. It started with the pressure of getting ready for a morning class—settling and feeding the dogs, clearing up the kitchen and preparing snacks, getting a good fire going in the woodstove, and cleaning and straightening the house. Then, because of one member, the class teetered on the edge of falling apart. That one member had fallen into spiritual bypass mode and knew for a fact that she was the one the universe had chosen to lead things, even though those things had little to do with the material being covered, which had to do with bringing spirituality into everyday life. Many in the class seemed totally bewildered by her contributions, and by the end of the session I was exhausted by the effort of constantly easing her pronouncements back from cloud nine. When everybody had left, I took Molly upstairs with me for a nap, and after she roamed about for ten minutes she was ready to be lifted up and have a good doze. At times like that, dealing with a dog going off its training didn't seem nearly as bad as dealing with a class member going full steam off the rails.

During afternoon recovery time we brought the three dogs over to the living room, and Liam was the one who, after a brief session of training, curled up on the couch with us. Other than that, I mostly just sat in the back room with all three, and Molly was the one who wanted to hang around and be held. During play periods it was now Molly and Liam who formed a lively team. When she was with Rowan Molly's Mae West side came out, which is why we had begun checking her "condition" frequently.

In the back kitchen the next morning Liam forgot himself and wet in the middle of the floor. He knew when he had done something wrong, though, because when I looked at it and then at him, he dashed for the den and huddled in a corner. Rowan was bursting with energy and enthusiasm, and when I took him over to the living room for his training session he outdid himself with cooperation. During the afternoon Pat continued to work on store records and then had to tend to things in town. I took Molly with me upstairs. She acted as though she didn't really want to be there, but when I took her from upstairs to downstairs, she sort of wanted to go back upstairs.

The next day was again pretty much procedure as usual, except that a cold snap was approaching and we all prepared to huddle. Nights had again become times of semi-doze, with the dogs arising at all hours to clear themselves out. That evening we watched part of a mystery with Liam curled up between us. Even though he had become even cuter than he had been, he still had times of forgetting his training. Earlier I happened to look in on them at the exact moment when he was dragging a wet paper across the floor. There was no way he could deny it, so he sat dejected in a corner and felt very, very sorry—at least for a few minutes—for what he had done.

Molly would still not respond well to training, but was content simply to be noticed and combed and held. She now weighed ten pounds and was filling out more solidly and had become even more of a joy to hold and carry around, in part because of her stillness and sense of presence when picked up. Even though Liam continued to be the cutest, Rowan the one most alert, responsive, and eager to please, and Molly the most mulish, it was Molly who was still, for me, the most special.

That night the cold snap arrived and the temperature dipped to twenty below zero. The house remained in the upper fifties all day, so we all huddled close to radiators. During the afternoon we brought down another rocking chair from upstairs to replace the one in the back kitchen, which now had an arm that kept falling off. Once the new one was in the room, Pat saw that it was dirty, so I went over it with a wet sponge that needed to be cleaned frequently. The dogs thought it was really exciting to get a new chair to investigate and start to chew on, and they forgave me for wiping off all the tasty bits. Then we added to their pleasure by bringing in a new, special dog bed to replace the blanket under the desk, and they went temporarily insane with sheer delight. After they settled down they all wanted to stretch out on it at the same time. For a while Molly tried to dig into it to make a nest, so I put an old blanket on top of it, and all three of them tested it out with a meditative chew. They stayed close to it for the rest of the day, not once going anywhere near their den.

Before supper Pat brought a bottle of white wine over to the back kitchen, which was the warmest room, and we sat with the dogs, who enjoyed the company and all the extra attention. Rowan was the one who romped about the most, still not knowing what to do with all his energy in the dead of winter.

Pat and I both noticed that Molly had again developed a slight odor, probably from more hormones kicking in. Even though she was only five months old, we were keeping a close watch on her. The two males were becoming more interested, and she was starting to egg them on in various embarrassing ways.

We were having real problems trying to take pictures of them. Our new automatic camera made a funny whirring sound when it was turned on and when we put it on zoom, and whenever the dogs heard it, they stopped doing whatever cute thing they were doing and dashed toward the camera. We didn't know what they thought it was, but no matter how long I held it and waited for them to strike a pose, the minute I raised it, over they came. We couldn't wait all that long either, because after a couple of minutes the camera would automatically whir and return to its default setting, which would again cause the dogs to leap up and rush over.

After a cold day and a dark, stormy, restless night, the next morning started with a contest between Pat and me for being the first—or maybe the last—to go downstairs. I surfaced around 8:00, and after the dogs cleared themselves out, I took them downstairs and made coffee while Pat remained in bed.

I wasn't sure whether that meant I had won or lost the contest.

Once the dogs were down and had finished running and playing, they all decided it was time for each one to stake a claim for a place on their new bed. The outside temperature had risen to twenty-two degrees, which was forty-two degrees warmer than the previous day, so even though it was snowing and sleeting, the house remained warm. During the day, when Pat had to be out, all three were well enough behaved that I was able to shovel the five inches of wet snow, bring in some wood, do dishes, and fix myself lunch. Pat returned in time to fix lunch for the dogs, after which I took Molly upstairs with me for a short nap. When Molly and I came back downstairs, Pat took a longish nap to try to ease a pain in her left side and an inflammation in the right side of her face near the hinge of the jaw.

Even though the poor dogs had another day with little excitement, they were remarkably good about it and remained alert. During the evening some snow *whumped* off the barn roof and all three were ready to do battle, even though they had no idea with what they would be doing battle.

5

Middle Adolescence

THE NEXT day marked the start of their thirteenth week with us on the thirteenth day and on a Friday in the middle of a January thaw with a full moon just around the corner. We took it to mean that the signs were good, although we weren't sure what they were good for because during the previous night the signs had been mixed. After I prepared the bedroom and returned for the dogs, Rowan came when called and I took him upstairs where he settled in with Pat. When I went back, neither Liam nor Molly paid any attention to my calling their names, so I had to drag them off their new rest area. Liam was so reluctant that he just went limp so that I couldn't get a good hold on him. Then there were further distractions all night long. Snow kept falling off the roof with great *whomps*, bringing them all to full alert. Then the wind came up such that something kept going *knk!* against the side of the house, which also brought them to full alert. At 2:30 Molly and Liam wet and did businesses, after which the sound of *knk!* continued until daylight.

The effects of the full moon became strongest the next day, and all three were again out of control until midafternoon, with wild barking, dragging wet papers around, and eating droppings. I tried to keep it all cleaned up while also helping Pat get ready for company, but it was a difficult day, partly because despite her aches and pains Pat was straight out busy fixing food and needing help, and partly because we felt that even though the people coming were dear friends and it wasn't their fault, they couldn't have come at a worse time. Pat did take a few minutes to stroll around the house with Rowan and urge him to walk up and down stairs, and we did have all three briefly in the living room, but the dogs were just one more task that needed doing. Then around 5:00 the company arrived, which at least changed the atmosphere, even though the dogs barked steadily and thoroughly messed up the back kitchen. For them it was another two steps backward.

The guests, Diane and Richard, had come to Vermont for cross-country skiing in nearby Craftsbury, but we doubted they'd find any snow because the previous day had become warm, the night had stayed warm, and that day the temperature was back in the fifties. We did have a good chat, snacks, and supper despite the dog distractions, and late in the evening they went to the B and B across the street.

The next morning they stayed at the B and B until about 10:30, then went for a two-hour walk while we took all three dogs outside briefly and let them roam around the side yard and enjoy the fifty-seven-degree day. The guests then visited with us until about 2:00, when Richard decided they really should move on to Craftsbury and we said our goodbyes. After supper we took Rowan to the living room without his leash, a move that pleased him greatly, and he even obeyed some of the commands. We had added "down" for stretching out flat, and he responded well. With the guests now on their way, the dogs became more agreeable and the general atmosphere now seemed much more relaxed.

The following day, the sixteenth, was again springlike, with temperature up to fifty-eight degrees, and all three had a good run outside. Back inside, Rowan was the one who came on his own when called, and we let him run freely about the living room. He had also mastered the art of going up the five steps from our front room, through the shop, and into the back kitchen, leaving Molly and Liam seething with jealousy.

All three continued their good behavior, and Rowan headed for my feet whenever he wanted to lie down. Even Molly improved, looking alertly toward me whenever I called her name. Whenever we watched a movie or the news, they roamed a bit and then settled down on the couch and on our laps. In the back kitchen they all now played "cardboard tube," even though by now the tube had definitely become subdued.

The next morning was quiet, heavily damp, and just above freezing. It began on a cheerful note, with Rowan engaging me in a "morsel attack," a game he had developed. He'd stand over me on the bed, pretend to growl, and start a friendly lunge toward me. Whenever I responded, he wiggled happily and would be at it again until I finally gave in and got up. After we were all up, fed, and sorted out, Pat had to go shopping, and when she returned she said that the car had developed some sort of problem. I took it down to Benny, but he had no idea what was causing it but told us not to worry. I didn't tell Benny that we hadn't been worried at all until he told us not to worry.

Later that day Rowan and Molly discovered the joys of a roll of toilet paper, spreading bits of practically the whole roll all over everywhere just before supper. And when I left them long enough to fix the bed in my study for night, they chewed the kitchen linoleum. Once they were upstairs Molly remained stubborn and independent, keeping her ears flat out in their "stupid" position. Thus ended the day when they were officially five months old.

The springlike weather continued with temperatures in the forties and lots of sunshine. The dogs remained in high-energy mode but cheerful. Their only error was that while Pat and I were alone in the living room, they ripped open their big dog pillow in the back kitchen and started messing around with the foam and wood chips, which put an end to their comfy sleeping place. And yes, we had another evening class, this time in the front room of the store. It went surprisingly well, and all the members also remained cheerful, possibly because we had begun to open the usual class material to a wider perspective. Pat watched the dogs during it—the longest she had been with them for a while—and she too noted that all three had grown and were now coming into their own. They too were moving toward a wider perspective.

During the next few days Pat experienced a pain in her back and had trouble getting up and about, so I did whatever I could and also, because the car continued making funny sounds, again took it down to Benny for a general going over, which involved a lube, oil, filter, and expensive tailpipe. After that the only funny sound I heard was the one Pat made when I returned home and showed her the bill.

The good news was that Molly had returned to her friendly mode and now stayed close by when I was with them in the back kitchen.

As the months passed I felt that maybe the time with the dogs wasn't a 40-day or an 80-day retreat but more likely a retreat of maybe 101 days, after which I'd plan to end an every-day journal and let entries become sporadic. In general the dogs continued to grow, their manes were coming in, their times of mature behavior were more frequent, and they were better about their bathroom needs. The main thing I now dreaded was the change from their being paper-trained in the house to taking care of all their needs outside.

My schedule had become pretty routine: except for brief episodes of house and yard duties, I was spending twelve hours a day in the back room with the dogs, ten hours a night in my upstairs study with the dogs, and two hours a day in the living room, mostly with the dogs. From time to time Pat asked me if my going into town would be a good chance to get away for a while, but I told her that just my having unrestricted use of the house sounded like a vacation. For Pat, who had access to the entire house, getting away meant going to town or driving an hour or so somewhere. I then figured that for those who drive around every day, getting away meant going to Florida or Arizona or such, and those who did that anyway cast their eyes toward foreign shores. Some friends who ordinarily travel a bit were planning a trip to Bali, and a member of our center who routinely traveled to Colorado and California was away for a week in Rome. So like much else, it was relative, and I continued looking forward to unrestricted use of the house.

Day 94 involved yet another morning class, which meant that Pat and I had a mad scramble to take care of dogs, clean up the house, clear a table in the shop, and prepare snacks. There never seemed time to sit quietly in order to gather one's thoughts ahead of time, and even with the wider perspective, the effort to move people forward in the classes was again beginning to seem a waste. That day was a case in point. One person acted as though he had never heard or thought about some of the things we'd been dealing with for ten years, so it was back to ground zero—or maybe just two steps backward. Then another member started praising a feel-good, superficial New Age book she had started reading, and some of the others picked up on it. I was familiar with the book and dared to express my unhappiness with it on all counts, and it was as though I had attacked their personal ancestry. It was clearly time for me to sit back, relax, and simply breathe, especially because I was also getting really tired of dealing with three shelties who insisted on taking steps backward.

It was true that Molly had been acting more friendly, but she had also taken a liking to dog droppings. She stood poised when one of the others did a business and then lunged for it despite my efforts to stop her. It was also true that Liam had become the one who would settle right down in the living room, but he also had episodes of uncontrolled barking at any unexpected noise or at anyone who visited us. Rowan, who was the most good-hearted and enthusiastic, was also becoming the rebellious teenager who would not mind and would become the most overbearing toward the other dogs. If, for example, I were to put Molly on the floor after holding her or carrying her somewhere, Rowan would be all over her in such an aggressive way that I'd have to hold him back. I suspected that no breakthroughs would happen by day 101.

The next day marked my first day out into the world in over three months. Pat had felt ill, so I made the rounds to Ames, Grand Union, the redemption center, and Agway. It took over three hours, but Pat didn't mind because it saved her the trip, and besides, I always brought home various items that she always felt she shouldn't buy, like doughnuts and pizza and such.

That morning I had also been busy with garbage, laundry, a dog run in the living room, and a mail run even before the trip into town. After I returned from town we ate a late lunch, had another dog run, did dishes, and took a nap. My being away for that long was something new for the dogs, and for the rest of the day whenever I left them, they barked and whooped around, knowing that I was somewhere nearby. If I took one of them with me, the others howled and fought. Finally I ended up in the back kitchen with all three curled up by my feet.

My notes for day 96 made clear why I was feeling it was time to draw the journal to a close: "This was neither a good day nor a bad day. It came, it went, there was a dusting of snow, nothing special in the mail, no trips anywhere, no great insights on anything, the dogs acted the way they usually do, and now it's time for bed."

The next day, another day of winter doldrums, things stayed on hold. I weighed the dogs: Rowan, 15 pounds; Molly, 11 pounds; Liam, 10 pounds. Like everyone else, Pat knew for a fact that Liam was the cutest of the three, and after he finished a meal she would hold him on her lap for a minute while he grunted. She also felt that his profile was the best, mostly because it had a smiling turn to it but also because he wagged his tail whenever possible. I had taken to calling him Doodoo for no good reason, but Pat thought that was unseemly.

Day 98, the end of their fourteenth week here, again marked two steps backward. They had reverted to wetting on the living room rug rather than using the box with papers or letting me know they had to go to the back kitchen. They still weren't all those things everyone told us shelties were supposed to be, and it again seemed as though the whole experiment of extended retreat had been mostly a waste. As with the center classes, there were moments of great satisfaction, and then suddenly it would be clear that little progress had been made. With both we were virtually back to square one.

Day 99 was also 10 days beyond their first three months here and the 155th day of their being anywhere, and they were back to being energetic puppies with only occasional episodes of being anything more than that. The afternoon was again a back-and-forth time of their settling down and then having to "go," with occasional periods of good-natured play. On the previous day the greatest anxiety occurred when I went to the newsroom and found no papers available, but to my relief the nice lady showed me where she had already set aside a small armload for me.

I was pleased that whenever I was away for a while, I returned to dogs that were genuinely happy to see me and ready to settle down by my feet. The only awkwardness was that at night Rowan had taken to sleeping by my head, which was okay except that he also liked to rearrange himself frequently so that I would have to wake up to lift him and shove him to one side, after which he would rearrange himself still further against another part of my body.

The next day was the first day of my wearing a bulky pullover sweater, and as usual with anything new, all three were very excited. I wasn't quite sure whether it was that sweater or me they wanted to be around. Molly especially found that she liked to be held so that she could curl up next to it. A little later, when they were all settled down around my feet, I thought I smelled a bit of business so got down on my hands and knees. That was too much for them, and they all climbed over me ready for a good tussle. It made me think that maybe they were learning to do what shelties were supposed to do after all. Then came evening. I left them to have supper with Pat, and they erupted into an all-out dogfight. Worse yet, it was over a bit of dog business that Rowan grabbed just as I arrived.

That episode tended to strengthen my feelings that they couldn't be left alone at all, that they weren't housebroken, that they hadn't developed any kind of rhythmic schedule, and that the whole house seemed to smell of dog pee and dog poop. And Pat was exhausted, making it all seem impossible.

The final day of this phase of the so-called retreat arrived, and along with it came another day of headache for me that refused to go away. Other than that the day was neither better nor worse than others. The dogs were older, but they would have been older no matter what. I thought that maybe the message of those 101 days was that there were no messages, that nothing really changes, no magical breakthroughs happen, and with the dogs it was just a case of more soggy papers to pick up and droppings to flush away and meals to fix. The dogs were really no better or worse than they had been, and their bad habits weren't improving. It wasn't their fault; despite the best of intentions and efforts, we obviously weren't meeting their needs. Pat felt that nothing additional could be expected from her with them in terms of their supervision or training, and my efforts seemed pointless. Obviously 101 days weren't nearly enough, and I knew that I still had to learn to sit and breathe.

February and March

By February 1, day 104, the dogs had taken at least half a step forward. Molly now lay by my feet and enjoyed being held and carried around. The white of her ruff had also grown out so that she looked quite distinguished. Rowan, still the independent adolescent male, stayed close to me and seemed aware of whatever I was doing. Like Molly, he enjoyed being combed, although his ruff looked windblown. Liam fought being combed and on occasion even growled. He was the one now most demanding of attention, sitting and barking whenever he wanted me to come to him. He had generally become tetchier, sometimes growling at the others and trying to start a fight.

The biggest weather change, a really deep freeze, began five days later, February 6, with the daytime temperature rising only to fourteen below zero. Since the long-range forecast was for more of the same with a bracing wind-chill factor, we closed off the big living room in the barn and brought plants and anything liquid into the front room. The dogs adjusted well even though they now mostly moped around, disappointed not to be able to run about in the living room or go outside. At night we all snuggled into or around extra blankets, with all three beasties stretched out by my neck or shoulder.

(2/12/95) Yes, we did have a cold snap up here; and yes, we did have high winds; and yes, it snowed a whole lot. How do we stand it? There are days—sometimes whole weeks—when we're not sure, and that's when we make two or three rooms snug and then try to ignore everything else. It's called going into torpor, and it's rather nice. We'd be in it even more except for the three rambunctious sheltie puppies who are almost but not quite six months old.

The thing with shelties is that even though they look like miniature collies, they're not. They were bred to be feisty little sheepdogs, and they view their world as preparation to tear around the Shetland Islands looking for stray sheep. It's a challenge to get used to their alert, ready-for-anything, full-of-action manner. If they do something bad or start to play too roughly and I slap the floor firmly with rolled-up paper, they just shout "Oh boy!" and leap to include me in their rompings. Pat says they see me as a big toy.

People who praise shelties always praise having one sheltie, as in "A sheltie is a good choice of dog [singular] for an older person." More than one and they urge each other on. Your outlook on life would take on a whole new slant if you could experience being in the same bed with all three of them at 4:30 when they suddenly hear the snowplow go by.

(2/19/95) The other night we watched a video of Ethan Frome, the movie filmed here in the Northeast Kingdom. It's a February film, a very good one which I'm sure would have received wider notice if it had been filmed in Sweden and had subtitles. I guess that's it . . . February up here is Bergmanesque. The dogs, all of whom had made three steps forward, have celebrated February by taking two steps backward. This is in addition to another observation that they always take steps backward around the three days during the full and new moons. For some reason it evidently throws them off just enough so that they revert to, well, loony behavior: hair-trigger wild barking at the slightest noise anywhere, plumbing misbehavior that doesn't bear thinking about, crazed yapping and howling if I leave them even for a few minutes. And in addition, Molly is thinking seriously of going into heat. Maybe we're leaving Bergman and moving toward Fellini. I'll have to practice a whole new accent.

Late February had arrived and the days were longer, the slant of light was different, and the daily temperature was sneaking upward. On the seventeenth the dogs were six months old, but even so, they still cavorted like puppies— chewing things, tearing around, putting up fusses. We made an opening in a wall to create a runway for them from the back kitchen, through the laundry room, and down three steps to our front room. They learned to use it whenever they wet and did business. Molly had least control, and several times she simply let loose with no warning in the front room. So if a period of time passed without her doing anything, I either carried her over or took her upstairs to my study.

Now that they had grown larger, their only problem at night was sorting all of us out on the bed. They were, however, now able to sleep through the entire night unless awakened by a snowplow or snow falling off the roof. In the morning they each took a solo turn on the papers, and after their breakfast I'd escort them over to the back kitchen for another cleaning out before opening the runway for them to gallop through on their own.

Because of cold weather we were all still in the front room with all the greenery, and the dogs noted that plants had soil. When they bit into it, they occasionally came up with stones, which they'd spit out. I hesitated to descend on them too rapidly for fear that they might swallow them.

Things had seemed pretty awful by the end of those first 101 days, but even with their occasional adolescent mishaps, all three were finally becoming more trustworthy.

6

Late Adolescence

AS THE three dogs approached the end of their adolescence, they now were becoming, well, shelties. According to one source, "The breed is known to be tremendously obedient and is characterized as docile with great intelligence." We keep reminding them of that, but for the most part they prefer not to listen.

Now that the six-months-old barrier had been passed, they were gradually coming into their own. No overnight breakthroughs, but little by little each one was, despite setbacks, averaging out into being a responsive individual. Liam was still especially responsive to dog droppings and went for them. I went for them, too, but for different reasons than Liam, who saw them as appetizers. When Liam was younger, our friends called him Piglet, and it fit. Then at odd moments we called him Doodoo, which also fit. At six months he was sure his name was Liam No!

The good news was that by the end of February all three dogs could be trusted enough to have the run of the house. When they had to go, they hurried through the runway to the back kitchen. They were also even more oriented to us exclusively, at best a mixed blessing because whenever anyone else appeared on the scene, they went into protective mode with much barking.

Molly now teased the others more frequently, so I needed to watch carefully because she was ready to go into heat at any time. Because of her teasing, Liam became a bit jealous of Rowan. Whenever I had to reprimand all three of them, he'd turn on Rowan as if to say, "See, it's all your fault!" Rowan, who now weighed seventeen pounds, had developed even more energy, too, and all three continued to be greatly excited about unfamiliar clothing, something different on the floor, or indeed anything new in the house. If I even made a strange sound, they were all over me.

The disappointment of those first 33-day periods and the 101 days had begun to lift. I finally realized that even though we were all still going through a process, we could not impose time limits on it. Part of the process seemed to be to develop patience, to have no expectations, and to take nothing for granted. Even so, I decided to keep thinking of the process as a retreat, this time extended to 1,001 days, by which time all the training and preparation would be completed. It was a serious consideration, because if accounts were correct, dogs were considered to be the guardians of the boundary between wildness and domesticity. It was humans who had caused dogs to evolve from wild animals to domestic companions, just as it was dogs who helped humans to develop from wandering hunter tribes to settled agrarian tribes. Not only that, but dogs were also understood to be guardians of the threshold between this world and the next and therefore were often stationed at dangerous heavenly crossroads and bridges. Theirs had become a symbiotic relationship with us, and with the three shelties much more of that was still waiting to be developed. Just as with humans, dogs could go through life half asleep and so needed to be awakened to their own significance. These shelties and their caretakers were approaching the end of their basic training, and part of this next period of retreat would be to help them wake up, just as their presence would help us to become more fully awake. In order to develop that potential, we had to understand their dogginess as only one form of their true being.

Other books corroborated this view. One of them, J. C. Cooper's *Symbolic & Mythological Animals* (Aquarian Press, 1992), said:

> The Avesta and other sacred books say the dog symbolizes sagacity, vigilance and fidelity and is the pillar of the pastoral culture. It must be treated with the utmost kindness and reverence. . . . The death of the body and the transit of the soul required the presence of a dog. . . . In creation the dog ranks next to the human. . . . As the dog can see spirits it can act as an intermediary between people in this world and the next and can also ward off evil spirits and protect from the powers of darkness. Dogs guard the Cinvat Bridge which must be crossed into the next world and where the good and evil are separated; they protect the righteous but do not stop the evil spirits from tripping up the bad, who then fall into the pit. . . .
>
> The dog is important in Celtic myth. . . . Dogs are associated with the healing waters and Nodens, God of Healing, could manifest as a dog. Dogs are also psychic animals and connected with divination and they are frequently metamorphosed people in Celtic lore. (75, 77)

These selections and others encouraged us to stay with our intent to keep the retreat process active.

Another bleak period began for all three shelties, however, about the middle of March. Spring was approaching, and their nervous activity increased with more running about, getting into things, and even doing businesses inside their den—something they had never done before. I couldn't trust them enough to leave them alone. Our car was also having extended work done at the garage, so neither of us was able to enjoy even a brief getaway drive. We had been invited to visit our friend Ellen on the Maine coast in June, but we had doubts. Pat would still have to fix the dog meals every day and be limited otherwise to whatever fit into Ellen's schedule, not to mention that Ellen was accustomed to our well-trained, cooperative collies. We doubted whether she'd be able to put up with three rambunctious shelties plus us in her cottage.

Ten days later the car was still at the garage in the middle of a motor job, and Pat and I were more than a bit frustrated. The dogs were, however, back to normal and had again become quite endearing. One night during this time I woke up with severe abdominal pain. As it became worse, my first impulse was to writhe on the floor and moan. I did not want to alarm Pat, though, so I remained quiet and moved about on the bed as little as possible. Whenever I did have to double up and change my breathing pattern, Molly and Liam either slept on or rearranged themselves.

Rowan was the one who sensed that I was not doing well. First he looked up at me, and then, while I lay on my right side, he came up and lay beside me, pressing like a warm compress against the hollow made by my chest and stomach. Soon the pain lessened, and I held him there all night long.

Even though I continued to be partial to Molly, I realized how much I valued Rowan's ongoing healing presence. He was now the one who showed the greatest capacity to become Responsible Dog.

(3/22/95) According to the calendar spring arrived shortly after nine on Monday evening. According to a glance outside, spring is buried somewhere under still-deep snow in the side yard. When I step in the snow on my way to the bird feeder, the inside of my moon boots (don't laugh; that's what they're called) become tightly packed in ice. When I later empty the moon boots out in the front room, the dogs attack the snow, thinking I collected it all solely for them.

The dogs now have the run of most of the house, which means in part that they now discover new things to eat. They've investigated the cracks between the wide boards in the store and found bits of things you ordinarily don't even think about. When the weather does admit to the inevitable and allows spring to arrive, then the dogs will begin to discover the fun of chasing and eating little things that fly and crawl. I guess it's something to look forward to.

On March 23 the dogs had their rabies shots, a requirement for their being licensed. We would rather not have had to do it, since we knew about the harmful possible side effects both short term and long range, but we had no choice. For the following five days we administered a homeopathic remedy to help them detox. Susan came to the house to give the shots and this time stayed for a two-hour visit while all three dogs remained on their very best behavior.

A week later, at the very end of March, spring finally arrived in the Kingdom. The sun again shone through the window over the sink in the back kitchen and made a bright square of light in just the right place on the floor. Liam found it and liked to spread out over most of it, occasionally looking up into the light. I used one of those times to study him more closely, and I first noted that his ruff had finally begun to come in, although parts of it still stuck out like tufts of grass. Whenever he now sat at attention and waited for a treat, his ruff puffed out. He lay such that I could observe the last two inches of his tail, which were bent at a right angle—probably from a birth defect—although it didn't seem to bother him at all. The tip of his tail was white, as was the ruff on his chest. All four feet were also white, the front ones up to the second big joint. The white continued like a collar just below his neck. His ears, which stood up like a fox's, were dark sable, and his face was light sable except for a spot of white on the left side of his muzzle near the nose.

Liam also now enjoyed spending part of each day as a lap dog. He might have been tearing around, egging the other two on or barking furiously at every imagined sound throughout the house, but then he would come over to Pat or to me, assume a bedraggled, worried look, and beg to be picked up and cuddled. He did, though, still have two bad habits we hoped he would get over. One, which he shared with the others, involved that wild yapping at the arrival of any visitor. Whenever we picked him up, he stopped, but then he still looked terribly worried. The other bad habit was his fondness for dog droppings unless I was around to stop him. If I checked the papers and found evidence of where a dropping had been, I'd smell his muzzle, and sure enough, it was always Liam whose mouth had the giveaway odor.

April and Onward

(4/17/95) One large (and it does loom large) problem is that all three are extremely territorial. They have pretty much the run of the house now, and they mostly behave well as long as everything goes just so. If a newcomer enters the house, though, they go into a period of wild barking; and if they're then shut in the back room, they continue the wild barking at the slightest sound from the interloper. If the dogs are free and the visitor sits without moving, the dogs will circle him or her and tentatively sniff and growl. If the seated person then dares to move a muscle, back comes the wild barking. They'll get over it; we all do as we steadily mature. I think I read that somewhere.

(5/3/95) The three dogs, now approaching their ninth month, are doing what sheltie puppies do, which is a combination of being adorable and being exhausting. Pat says they're now in the equivalent of the Terrible Twos.

May 8 marked their two hundredth day with us. Their progress had been slow, but on the average they were behaving much better than they had in March. With spring now present, they spent more time outside in their new pen on a section of the lawn behind the store kitchen. Two sides of it were fifty-foot lengths of wire fence four feet high with a gate large enough to move a mower through or to enter from the rest of the backyard. The other two sides were outside walls of the back kitchen and the redone barn. The back kitchen door and the door in the big living room both opened onto it, and the dogs now had about two thousand square feet of protected area in which to run about.

They were also going through the trauma of learning to wet and do business outside. Liam had caught on after only a few days, and Molly was more or less catching on. Rowan had reached the point where he felt that he was not supposed to wet or do business anywhere, so he'd hold it all in until finally it emerged in a torrent wherever he happened to be. We watched closely, and whenever he acted ready to go we put him either outside or, in bad weather, in the store kitchen with papers. He'd go then, but he'd feel really bad about it. If the other two then saw inside papers, they'd think, "Oh, good," and use them even when the outside door was open.

When the car was repaired we began to take the dogs car riding. At first it was difficult, and Molly trembled most of the time during any trip to town. Once she became used to it, she preferred to curl up on the floor by the back seat, and Rowan found room on the floor between the two front seats. Liam divided his time between the front and the back. We took them along to a book sale in Hanover, two hours away, and they were good for the entire twelve-hour-plus time. We took turns going to the sale, and I tried my best to lead them on walks and get them to wet and do business, but they wouldn't do it. That trip happened before we had fenced in any outside area, which meant that after they arrived home, they proceeded to wet copiously all over the back kitchen floor. In fact, Rowan was so plugged up that he couldn't go, and then when he finally had no choice he didn't make it to the back kitchen and wet all over the store floor, the front room, and the steps going up to the shop. The fenced-in area now made a huge difference, but we knew it would still be a slow learning process for the dogs before they felt it was quite all right to "go" outside.

(5/22/95) The three dogs enjoy this exuberant spring and like to go outside into their new fenced-in area. We hesitate to let them out when it's wet or rainy, because it's no easy task to dry off a soggy sheltie. We've started what will be a long process: training them to go for a walk on a leash and take care of plumbing needs at our convenience. We're still at the beginning stages of

convincing them that it's really all right to wet outside. Given the choice, they'll play outside and then run in to relieve themselves on the papers, as they've done all winter. If we pick the papers up, they suffer, because they know there's no place to do anything. Liam is sort of catching on, but Rowan takes it to the point that if there are no papers inside he'll allow himself to become all plugged up, and then suddenly he'll let loose no matter where he is, panic, and run the length of the house, leaving a trail that winds through three or four rooms. He knows that one doesn't wet outside.

By the fourth week of May Rowan was still in a terrible state about tending to his needs. He used indoor papers if we put them down, but whenever we put papers down outside on the grass, he became totally bewildered and didn't know what to do. During one evening, after ninety minutes of agony outside, he ran upstairs and wet on the papers in the study. Molly had sort of caught on, wetting inside if papers were around and doing so outside if that's where she happened to be when she needed to go. If she needed to go inside and there were no papers around, she'd simply squat. Liam seemed to be the only one who really caught on and gave us no trouble.

Molly was still her usual self, although Pat did admit that she now showed more individuality. She said that Molly's eyes indicated there was indeed a personality in there. Molly was now up to fourteen solid pounds and was the one who most liked to run with great energy. Except for her hysterical barking whenever anything different appeared or happened, she was the quiet one—unless, of course, she was bedeviling the two male dogs.

By early June we had phased out walking them with their leashes on collars, since they had been chewing on them, and moved on to harnesses, which they now wore whenever they went out with us. The weather had turned generally iffy, but I took the dogs outside no matter what. Liam continued to be the best trained, Molly still wet on urgency and without warning, and Rowan wasn't wetting so much as wetting his pants. He wet because he couldn't hold it anymore, and he'd leap and bolt when it happened. I had to walk him often, because motion was the only thing that loosened him up so anything would happen. I had to keep him confined to the leash inside, too, because indoors he'd still run around in a panic, wetting all over everything.

Things now looked increasingly grim regarding a trip to Maine. There was no back kitchen with papers at Ellen's, the weather was varied, there was always heavy dew, and there were hordes of vicious mosquitoes. And Ellen still harbored memories of our well-behaved collies.

But after the arrival of June the dog situation improved and all three took several steps forward. Rowan had already learned to go upstairs on his own, and on Thursday the eighth Molly finally convinced herself that she could go up a flight of stairs too. Until then I had forced her up by pushing her or by pulling her by her harness, but on that day she went step-by-step, carefully standing sideways on each step before stumbling to the next one. Then, after a couple of awkward tries, she could do it with no trouble. Within a few days she was going upstairs on her own whenever she could dream up an excuse. Liam was the only holdout, and he still went limp whenever I tried to push or drag him up the stairs.

On the tenth they had their first genuine obedience lesson from Muriel, who showed us how to walk them with a choke collar. She took all three through "heel" and "stay" and then had me do the same. After an initial wild balking, Molly caught on and did it the best of all. Rowan also caught on and, according to Muriel, looked the most attentive. On succeeding days the only problem was that he would heel so close to my leg that both of us sometimes stumbled. Liam was the only one slow to catch on. He'd balk, wouldn't respond to the tug of the collar, would sit so that he ended up being dragged and choked, and whenever the pull of the leash eased, he'd roll over on his back and look helpless and terrified.

Their transition to wetting outside was beginning to average out toward success, although they still had to learn how to let us know when they needed to go. Once outside, they'd wet where I led them, except that with Rowan it was still panic wetting. Rowan and Molly were still uncertain about pooping outside and did so only if they couldn't hold it any more. The only one who had no problems was, once again, Liam.

We had rearranged the master bedroom upstairs so that instead of two single beds, we had two box springs and mattresses together on the floor and a king-sized futon spread over them. That gave enough room so that all five of us could sprawl out more or less comfortably. The dogs, who until now had been crowded onto a single bed with me in my study, thought it was all quite nice. And once they were up in the morning they could now hold it until I let them into the outside pen to wet, and by late morning they'd be ready to go on a serious bathroom walk.

All three were also showing more interest in being "family." We had again opened and resettled the big living room and they were now given the run of the house, although they preferred to stay close to us even when they played together. They still made a racket whenever anyone came, but their behavior improved once visitors stayed for a while. We reminded ourselves that they were still a small pack of ten-month-old, strong-willed shelties and that they would continue to reinforce each other's wild behavior.

During late June we did decide, with Ellen's encouragement, to make that trip to her cottage, and it turned out much better than we had expected. The dogs cooperated well during the six-hour trip, and Ellen greeted them warmly and thought they were dear things. Once inside, they ran about with big smiles as they explored every room. They had no trouble taking care of themselves outside, and after a couple of mistakes the first day they caught on and made no more errors inside, probably because I took each one for a walk around an area of field and roadway seven or eight times every day.

During each day we all went on car trips. At Otter Point in Acadia National Park they were unimpressed with the ocean, but they did like to walk the ocean trail. Each one had a harness and leash, which meant that by the time we finished each walk all three leashes would be braided together in a complicated manner. Whenever we approached people on the trail, the dogs were very good, but if we were at our spot on the Point and anyone approached us, they put up a terrible fuss, since the Point was now their territory.

At night we arranged them on Ellen's guest bed with us, Rowan at the foot, Molly in the middle, and Liam up by the pillows. Once settled, they stayed in place all night long. We were usually up before Ellen, and I'd take them for their early walks, during which time they cleared themselves out thoroughly. A little later, when Ellen arose, they'd at first have a few words with her, but she was very good-natured about it, and by the time the visit was over, they'd just look her way and think, "Oh, Ellen's up."

When we returned home, we discovered to our relief that whenever they now had to tend to themselves, they actually asked to go out or would go to the outside door and look distressed. I'd let them out and all three, even Rowan, would do their wets or businesses with no hesitation.

A week or so later, on Tuesday, the Fourth of July, Molly finally went into heat, and Liam and Rowan had problems adjusting to it. Molly's main change was that she paid even more attention to the other two, sometimes being provocative and at other times being furious. The two males went a bit bonkers. Rowan did not want to leave her alone and would cause a commotion if separated from her. He mostly wanted to sniff and lick. Liam did the same, so that if he got

close to her, he followed behind her (or followed her behind)
like an appendage, nose firmly in place. He also began to wet
seemingly nonstop, leaving his mark all over the house. On
top of that, by the seventh we were in the middle of a re-
cord-breaking heat wave with muggy storms every day. At
night I slept with the two males downstairs while Pat stayed
upstairs with Molly. During the day I kept Molly near me
on a leash so she wouldn't be out of my sight with the two
males. At first she balked at the arrangement, but after a few
days she accepted it and even enjoyed it, so that whenever I
removed her leash for a while, she growled and barked at me
to put it back on.

One positive outcome of Molly's heat period was that Liam
finally learned to walk upstairs by himself, although the
method used to train him could be regarded as unconven-
tional. While holding Molly, I took him to the bottom of the
stairs. Then I held Molly in front of his nose and slowly moved
her from step to step. Liam was determined to keep his nose
close to Molly's behind, so he managed to move from step
to step until we reached the second floor. He was somewhat
disappointed when I then carried Molly away, but from then
on he had no trouble climbing the stairs all by himself.

*(8/1/95) Molly has been experiencing a period of heat. She final-
ly decided to do so a few weeks ago, fortunately not until after
we returned from Maine instead of in the middle of Acadia National Park. All she did was act like herself, only more so. Rowan
was ready to knock down walls to reach her, because he knew
what was what. Liam's response to Molly was somewhat different: whenever she wambled up to him and gave him her "Hello
there, big boy" routine, he whimpered and dribbled. The heat
period lasted about two weeks, and things are fortunately back
relatively to normal. Pat was more exhausted from it than I was,
but Pat never taught high school, where there are always several
young ladies in the middle of periods of heat.*

Tuesday, the first day of August, was an auspicious time, the

303rd day of the three shelties being with us. The first round of 101 days had been a real trial for all of us, and the second and third rounds were times of transition. We thought of each round as one more turning in the labyrinth of this now-extended retreat, with all three dogs still going through the process of becoming. They were all house-trained, although they still needed to work out what kind of signal to give us whenever they needed to go out. Every two hours I let them into their enclosed area, just in case, and they tended to themselves as needed, after which I'd stroll around and hunt for businesses, which I then picked up with an old leaf and placed in a plastic container. Usually once a day I also took them for leash walks around a complicated trail in our large backyard and had them heel and sit and stay, although Rowan was the only one who regularly took to commands.

Rowan was still the big oaf filled with energy, but he tried the hardest to be Noble Dog and still chose to lie by my feet inside. Molly became in some ways the most caring of the three. She'd stay nearby and be alert, not because I'd tell her to, but because she wanted to. She didn't try to crowd in for attention the way Rowan did, but she was now wiggly happy whenever I gave her my attention. She also had the best sense of play. She still had her bossy side, but I suspected that it was all an act.

On Sunday the thirtieth we had a bit of worry with Liam. He started vomiting, and Susan, our vet, advised keeping him off food for the rest of that day and then slowly easing him back to his regular meal over three days. His tender tummy may have been caused by a four-day visit by Kathy, a friend of Pat's. She and Pat had not seen each other for years, and with all the catching up and hosting, it ended up being a pleasant but hectic time with irregular feeding and bedtime schedules. For Liam the change was all too much, and it was shortly after Kathy left on Sunday that he started being sick. For a while we had to keep him mostly away from the others so that he'd remain calm. He didn't mind at all and mostly just slept in my study while the other two stayed nearby on the other side of a barrier in the doorway. They didn't seem to resent it, but they did want to remain close. At night we did keep all five of us together, which worked out all right and kept any of them from feeling excluded. Bit by bit Liam returned to his regular self, but it took a while with many naps along the way.

By early August the dogs made it clear that they were still youngsters by reverting to house-wetting and barking. I continued to take them for their regular walks outside, but now they did nothing until they returned inside. On the fourth, when we had visitors, they were so wild that we had to shut them in our small back screened room. When we let them into the living room, Molly proceeded to sniff the newcomers, walk to the middle of the rug, and wet, much to the amusement of our visitors. The backward turn of behavior made for a challenging week or two.

Liam was still the most sensitive of the three, although all of them still went wild through the house at the slightest excuse. We now gave Liam his meals in a separate room, because otherwise he bolted his food and then tried to attack the others. At other times he growled menacingly and circled the other two, and sometimes for no reason he turned on Rowan and attacked him so fiercely that we had to drag him away. Susan told us that this was normal behavior and that they were still working out who was the alpha dog. It seemed clear that Liam was pretty well convinced that the honor should fall to him.

At night all three now stayed downstairs with me while Pat got ready for bed, and when I headed up they came along without fuss and found a comfortable place on our bed. Liam had his own little pillow between those of the two humans, and he mostly stayed there. Molly usually found a place mid-bed, next to either Pat or me. Rowan slept either on the floor or at the foot of the bed. In the morning they waited while I got up and dressed and then, after I put on their harnesses, they all came downstairs with me. I'd then let them out to their pen and they'd take care of themselves, then come in and play until breakfast.

(9/9/95) The three dogs are all healthy and cheerful. Bit by bit they are becoming what shelties are supposed to be: loyal, sensitive, obedient. They're also strong-willed, stubborn, and xenophobic. And it's still true that three shelties are nine times more challenging than one sheltie. At this point, though, we cannot imagine having any number of shelties except three. So there you are. Rowan is the loyal, energetic one who always stays close by me. Liam, the little one, tries to be bossy and feisty but ends up being the cute, perky, cuddlesome lap dog. Molly remains, as always, Molly.

7

Young Adulthood

DURING AUGUST Pat developed a bad bronchial ailment, and I became the chief everything for about two weeks. The dogs had to stay out of the big bedroom, so they spent their nights with me in the study. For the most part they were now with no one else except me around the clock, which was okay, but it made them even more clannish.

By mid-September they were particularly stressed when a series of strangers entered the house and property but remained out of their reach. That was when an electrician tramped around upstairs rewiring the old apartment and relocating its fuse box. Then right after that Ken, a general handyman, spent a day doing outside painting and fixing of siding in their usual pen area, and that same evening our doctor, Denise, showed up for a visit. It all became more than they could handle, and they became so wild that I had to keep them out of the living room. By now, though, they had matured enough to know that they had gone too far, and when I fed them supper they minded their manners with each other. Afterward, when I brought them in one by one to say hello to Denise, they acted as good as possible.

Their mealtimes now required complicated maneuvering. I would first put down the plates for Rowan and Molly in the kitchen, shut the doors, and put Liam's plate on a little stand in the living room. Then I'd return to Rowan and Molly and, when Rowan was finished, I'd pick him up and carry him into the living room to allow Molly time to finish at her leisure. I would pick up Liam's plate and put it to one side and put both of the males outside in their pen while I went back to check on Molly. She briefly had the run of the house before going out with the males. After a clearing out they all came back in. It became a matter of routine, but I still looked forward to the time when all three would be able to eat together in the same room.

By mid-October we were approaching the first anniversary of their being with us, and I recalled how often during the previous year I had to be in the same room with them around the clock. Now, a year later, there were endless householder duties in addition to the dog work. The back kitchen area was in the process of being renovated. The carpenters had finished putting in a new window over the sink, and now it was a matter of laying new tiles over the old, used-up linoleum, a job mostly done by Pat. We knew that when winter arrived, the back kitchen would become a well-used area again with the advantage that the dogs, now well trained, could go outside to tend to themselves.

The rest of the year passed in a blur, with all three dogs cheerfully continuing to become themselves: Molly chunky and bossy, Liam feisty and cuddly, and Rowan the elegant and loyal galoot. It seemed as though no time at all passed before over two feet of snow had accumulated, and all three now loved it. Every day I had to shovel that enclosed area, since otherwise they wouldn't have been able to navigate in it. The section under the eaves of the barn remained unshoveled, though, so that they wouldn't be caught under falling ice and snow. That section was also portioned off with chicken wire soon buried under the snow, and the edge to which I shoveled served as a natural barrier.

The dog that was now bedeviling me the most when nature called was, of course, Molly. She didn't ask unless she was serious, as in Right! Now! She chose to become serious at times when everyone else was nicely settled down, but that was Molly. She might have been outside fifteen minutes earlier and not done anything, but that wouldn't matter. Now she really had to go.

The two males now wet every time they went outside, and if too much time went by, Rowan had learned to come over and paw me. Their plumbing was all very regular, as was their food: oatmeal and cottage cheese with supplements and olive oil in the morning, buttered toast with honey at noon, and rice with either cottage cheese or egg or tofu or meat in the evening. Molly was now up to 14 pounds, Liam was about 12 pounds, and Rowan weighed in at around 21 pounds.

They were partway through their second round of 333 days, and now Liam was bonding to Pat even though he remained the most independent of the three and still tried to assert himself the most. I had to continue feeding him separately in the living room because he insisted on growling and snapping at the others.

Liam and Molly now played together fairly roughly. She'd grab a mouthful of his ruff and drag him around the floor and shake him, but he didn't seem to mind. In general Molly had become the one most full of play. If either of the two males were to be pushed out of the way by a foot, they'd go off somewhere else, but if Molly were pushed, she'd think "Oh boy!" and turn it into a game. She was also beginning to develop her Nurse Molly side. When all three were on the bed and either Pat or I coughed loudly, Liam would move away, Rowan would look up and then go back to sleep, and Molly was now the one who would come over with a very concerned look to see if everything was okay.

Rowan continued to stay close to me during the day, usually not more than a couple of feet away. If I scolded him for anything, he was crushed. Two weeks earlier, when he had been inside for a while, I shut him up because of visitors. In his outrage at being shut up, he lost control and wet the rug. When I found it and reprimanded him, he slunk to the opposite side of the room and shook uncontrollably. Pat was a bit worried, and only after a session of reassurance did he stop shaking and settle back to looking woebegone.

They still enjoyed a "wild" time, usually in the afternoon, and ran and barked at every sound. They also still barked furiously whenever anyone came to the store or—heaven forbid—came over for a visit. The good news, however, was that they now calmed down sooner and were more responsive to discipline. Molly and Liam adjusted the most quickly to newcomers, but Rowan still skulked about and growled.

In mid-January the temperature dropped to five below during the day and twenty-three below at night, so we again closed off the living room, taking the plants and musical instruments once again to the front room, and the dogs had a difficult time whenever they had to go out to their enclosed area. Liam had the most trouble at first, because he had become used to taking his time wetting, doing business, and sniffing around. He tried doing all that the first really cold morning, then realized that his feet hurt, that he couldn't walk, and that the door was a long way away. Halfway back to the door he scrunched up, sat in the snow, and looked my way as if to say, "It's all over for me; say goodbye to everybody." Only after I spoke very firmly did he drag himself to the steps, force himself up them, and come into the room, where I then held him until he was warm enough to make believe that it had all been nothing at all.

Within a short time all three learned to go out, immediately do whatever they had to do, and tear back in. One day Molly took longer than usual, and partway back she sat in the snow and tried to raise both front feet at the same time. That didn't work, so she raised one after the other. I had to speak to her firmly, too, before she hopped to the door. When they were inside I had to keep a closer eye on them because whenever they now teased to go out, they really meant it.

With a smaller space inside and no place to run, they suffered from cabin fever and fussed a lot. Pat and I had by now become fully recognized as part of the pack, and they were very upset if any part of it became separated from the rest. When we all sat in the front room, they huddled close, and if I had to go uptown, Rowan would first act wild and then sit and shake.

(1/24/96) We have a fenced-in area for the dogs in the side yard, and two house doors open into it. One of these doors, the one into the barn/living room, is used in the summer; the other one, diagonally opposite in the old kitchen, is for winter use. The dogs can therefore enter the house in any season and be cozy and warm. After every snowfall (in December it snowed for 28 of 31 days) I go out and shovel.

The three companions have now pretty much reached their full growth and are working hard (and are being worked hard) to develop what will turn out to be their unique personalities. As a small pack they are lively, cheerful, and loyal. If we need to be elsewhere for a few minutes, they mourn our leaving, and then we return to a great bumbling tumult of happy wiggling and cavorting as each one shoulders the other two out of the way to be the first to greet us.

Molly is probably the most independent of the three, although every now and then she torments me unmercifully. She's the only dog I know who will literally knock a book or magazine out of your hand if you try to ignore her. She behaves like that when she wants something, although we don't always know what in particular it is she wants. If she's hungry but instead we take her out, she'll cheerfully go out but then afterwards will go back to bedeviling us until we get it right. She probably thinks we're terribly slow learners.

Rowan is becoming more definitely the Loyal Companion. Only rarely is he ever any distance from me, and if I'm in a chair, he's usually lying against my leg. Whenever we have company, he sits alertly at my feet, eyes fixed upon the interloper. When we're alone and he's in repose, he often has a look of great sadness. He wants to be a really good dog.

Liam is becoming the feisty little guy. When he was younger, he had random patches of long hair sprouting out from his short hair. Now he's a dignified, thoroughly longhaired thirteen-pounder who well deserves his title of Wee Beastie. He's the one who will take on anything, no holds barred. He'll spend time being a guy among guys, but then after a while he'll ask to be picked up and cuddled. At those times the Wee overcomes the Beastie.

By the end of February spring was almost in the air. The dogs didn't mind the outdoor chill, and when weather permitted, they chased each other around their pen and took their time coming back in.

A January thaw and February warm-up brought a bit of rain. Molly especially disliked it and couldn't understand why I didn't do something to make it all better. Whenever she had to go really badly, she'd come only partway to the door and then droop. I'd have to pick her up, lift her out to the back steps, and give her a little shove. Then she'd go a bit further under her own steam and tend to herself.

Molly also completed her second heat period, and after three weeks of being Molly Meek and mostly confined to my study, she made up for lost time by terrorizing Rowan and Liam. Earlier, when they realized that they couldn't get to Molly, they practiced howling like wolves and, when that didn't produce her, they decided it was each other's fault and spent long periods of time circling each other and growling. Then they lost their appetites and decided that the only alternative to Molly was to waste away with fond farewells. When Molly finally did reemerge as Queen of the Jungle, they retreated in a state of bewilderment.

The personalities of all three continued to unfold in two separate ways, first by their developing well as a pack of three (or five, counting us), and second as becoming companion dogs. Liam was still the feistiest, and I now called him

Wee Beastie as a matter of course. Rowan, although gentle, remained the most jealous, and Molly was now more quiet although still the biggest tease.

Molly had become even more chunky. Pat thought it was because of her body structure, but for whatever reason, she was now a solid little thing. She was also slowly becoming more bonded to me. At night she usually stayed on the bed by me until morning, and during the day she frequently wanted to be held or made much of, even more so than Rowan.

In a way the bonding of all three was a bit of a challenge. If Pat arose first, the dogs became excited and went downstairs with her, but that was their limit. None of them would go outside unless I was downstairs too. If Pat came back upstairs, all three followed her up and leaped on the bed to bedevil the daylights out of me until such time as I decided to arise. Then they'd all tease to go outside.

The center classes were also going well, and new people included a doctor with a Catholic background, a young fellow who knew Arabic and had converted to Islam, and two who had developed a connection with the downstate Mevlevi Sufi center, all giving added richness to the weekly gatherings. We now met in the old upstairs apartment area above the store, where center people had cleared a space, added a rug, and brought cushions. They took well to these tasks, and we now had much more conversation each time, refreshments partway through, more music, and one session each month totally dependent on their own contributions.

By the first week in March we all experienced the March blahs, which were different from the February blahs because the days were noticeably longer and the temperature was inching toward the no-longer-freezing mark. The dogs were bursting with energy and wanted to run about and go places, but even so, they were now unbelievably good. In the morning, when they decided that I had stayed in bed long enough and they really had to go, all three returned upstairs and quietly waited until I made some movement. Then they greeted me as if they knew for a fact that I really meant to get up.

Molly was now working on another aspect of her personality, the Sensuous Sheltie, and increasingly liked to be noticed and fussed with. When I petted and cuddled her, she looked very thoughtful and gave occasional grunts. Then, when she had had quite enough, thank you, she'd move slightly away and curl up. Whenever she had to do something serious, like tend to herself or have something to eat or play "toe" with me, she demanded attention. Little by little I learned her language.

Liam grew into an elegant puffball. He had become very responsive to us, and if we so much as looked at him when he was lying down, he gave us his full attention and wagged his tail. At those times the Wee overcame the Beastie, especially if he wanted to be picked up and cuddled. The Beastie most clearly came out at mealtimes, when he still growled unmercifully at the others. He had also taken on the job of guard dog downstairs and roared his challenge whenever anyone dared to walk by the house or turn a car around in our driveway.

Rowan still tried his best to be Good Dog, and at mealtime he now kept his distance from the others after he finished his bowl, and he waited until they were done before checking to see if they had left any tasty bits. The problem was that he was bursting with energy and could become quite rough with the others during play times.

(4/3/96) We're about halfway through the 1,001-day program. I'm referring to our three dervishes-in-training, of course. They completed the first 333 days—the physical part of it—with flying colors, and now they're working on (or wrestling with) the personality part of it. They're becoming increasingly dear companions, each in increasingly individual ways. As a group they've decided we're all one pack and that I am pack master. One result

is that the most effective discipline I now give is a bark and a stare. I have to be careful, though, because if I happen to, say, sneeze, they stop everything, look at me, and begin to wilt. It's not easy being a pack master.

Pat and I have been teaching Molly how to howl—you know, Aro-o-o-o-o-o! She catches on well, and from time to time the two of us go at it. Molly in turn urges the others. Now, when they're over yonder and I'm not, instead of barking like crazy they're just as likely to all set up a mournful howl. It's really quite lovely.

By the last week in April spring had definitely arrived, and the last lingering bits of ice on the ground melted away. The previous week's temperatures had been in the sixties, and even though the dogs took exception when we were outside and they were inside, we spent several days raking out all the areas of the yard and gardens that had things in them beginning to grow—many, many cartloads of leaves, straw, and old grass. We were in the nick of time, too, because then the weather turned cold and wet and things began growing like crazy.

(5/1/96) We took the three companions with us to the Five Colleges book sale. I had thought that I would spend most of the day in the car minding dogs, but the dogs were, so to speak, gooder than good. They told me they'd be quite all right by themselves. So I got to do everything and go everywhere. They sank into a sort of patient torpor, and periodically I roused them to go walkies and do whatever they had to do.

I don't know what went on in their minds about where we would end up, but they were totally surprised at the end of the day to discover that we had arrived home. For about two hours after our return they cavorted about with big smiles on their faces.

A week later Pat had an incident that gave us all pause. She had gone to a workshop, and because of sudden dizziness and queasiness she was barely able to make it home. Although we dowsed that whatever it was would pass, when Denise, our doctor, saw her, the first thought was that Pat should go immediately for a CT scan, especially since Denise was leaving the next day for a trip abroad. Pat asked her what the problem could possibly be. We ourselves then dowsed, and Denise gave permission to call our dowsing mentor, Terry Ross, from her office. Terry agreed with our dowsing about the situation, that it was most likely an inner-ear problem and not a stroke, and so we returned home. Sure enough, that's what it was and the problem gradually eased away.

Until that inner-ear problem was gone, however, I was again the one in charge of household duties as well as of dogs, who by now cooperated really well. They were aware of the situation and responded readily to my commands. They also wanted to add their help to anything Pat or I did. Whenever we put out birdseed on the window ledge, they leaped over to the window all excited and tried to be a part of the activity. They also continued to wait until I was up and about in the morning before asking to go out. If I did stay in bed too long, they now crowded onto the bed and on general principles urged me to arise. After they went outside for their morning wets, they waited in their places by their food bowls while I finished fixing their breakfast.

When breakfast was over they'd all go outside again and do businesses, and when they came back in Molly would have one of her Molly Moments on the couch, growling and throwing herself about. The rest of the time they kept me company while I tended to various household duties. By lunchtime they'd be really hungry and polish off their lunches in about ninety seconds. Liam would almost finish and then stand and growl. I'd pick him up, hold his plate, and let him lick the rest up while all the time he continued to growl. Following another plumbing trip outside, they'd enjoy a "wild" period inside with lots of barking and running about. There was nothing naughty about it, just lots of liveliness and noise. Their supper was then followed by another trip outside, with still another one just before we all headed upstairs to bed.

All their meals continued to be handmade with breakfasts of oatmeal, cottage cheese, and supplements; lunches of toast, butter, and honey; and dinners of rice, vegetables (usually carrots and peas), more supplements, and either chuck roast or eggs or cottage cheese.

We were relieved that they had each other to play with. We felt that even though it might hold back their full bonding with us, it kept them more enthusiastic, happy, and healthy.

The other chief event of the first half of May was our purchase of another car. We looked all over for a used one in good condition and found a really nice one. It was a bit more expensive than we had planned, but the dealer worked it out so that if we gave up our wild living habits and had no other expenses whatsoever for the next three years or so, we might just possibility be able to pay for it.

The following five weeks were all routine. It was also the first time in years that we hadn't been in Maine during the third week in June, and we discovered that Maine wasn't the only place where there were mosquitoes. The downside was that it was a damp time swarming with all sorts of bugs. The upside was that we did get to see a number of flowers bloom that we hadn't been around to see in years.

The center classes continued routinely well with their enlarged perspective. Pat gave a series of talks on Ibn 'Arabi, during which I played my part with confrontations regarding the nitty-gritty of the Sufi perspective as opposed to the feel-good stuff that generally draws people. The group rather enjoyed it, especially since by now each class included three alert shelties.

The dogs, although sweet and loyal, still took their periodic two steps backward with intense barking, general restlessness, and occasional mutual jealousy. In the morning they continued to wait until I was up and about before they went outside. For some reason they needed to know that I was right there to oversee them. It was sort of endearing but not really, because if I had to be off somewhere, I felt that they might put themselves into a state before they could make it outside.

We had set up a new king-sized bed upstairs in the redone barn, and at night Molly and Rowan stayed on it with us. Liam would stay for a while and then, being the independent one, would go onto a floor pillow. If I decided to remain up for a while, all three would stay downstairs with me. If I lingered there too long, Molly would draw my attention to the time by leaping up, knocking aside whatever I was reading, and urging me to come to bed for heaven's sake. All three would then perk up and follow me through the house to the stairs.

A trip with them to Plainfield and Montpelier surprised us because they were so good. They did bark like crazy for a while at people getting out of or into cars when we were parked at the Berlin Mall, but they responded well when I told them to stop and, to my surprise, they refrained from further barking.

Three weeks after that trip the moon struck again and marked another step backward for the dogs. Their barking grew more uncontrollable, and they took to growling more frequently at each other. If I picked up Rowan when he was in that mood, he growled menacingly at me. During that time a friend stopped for a visit, and in the middle of it one of the three wet on the front rug, something they never did any more.

Incidents like that caused me to feel that even though all three were really sweet and as loveable as ever, there were moments when they weren't very likeable.

Early in July, when the weather was clear, we purchased 300 feet of wire fencing and chicken wire and metal posts and expanded the enclosed area out back. When we were done the area extended from their old enclosed area on the north side of the house, around the wild roses, past the storage shed, along the base of our hill to the east over to the apple trees, then around the blackberry bushes, and down to a pile of wood from the cut-down tree and across the yard to the south corner of the house. The chicken wire was for numerous "gates" so that the humans could get into and out of the enclosed area to do things like tend to the gardens and mow and take out trash. At first the dogs didn't know what to make of the new arrangement and weren't sure whether or not they were really supposed to be there without their leashes, but with our encouragement they soon thoroughly explored the new area and discovered the joy of taking turns leading the pack and running flat out around the open areas and various complicated paths we had made around the back gardens.

By July 23 Molly was again in heat and this time we saw to it that she wore special panties made especially for dogs in her state. She also needed to be kept under watch for about three weeks, which would also mark the end of Phase Two of this extended retreat. There had been only a little bleeding, and although the two males hadn't been going bonkers, they were teasing more to go out or to be noticed, and Liam was beginning to smell male-doggy.

We were relieved when the backyard fencing was completed, because all three could now explore every inch of the open area at their leisure and run along all those complicated paths I kept mowed around the gardens. We weren't running around them quite so much ourselves, though, because the warm, muggy weather encouraged mosquitoes so much that we enjoyed the yard for only about ten seconds at a time.

On the twenty-first, just before Molly's heat period, we all went down to the annual quilt show in Northfield, and I again stayed with the dogs while Pat looked at the exhibits. The weather was slightly cool with fleecy clouds, and again the dogs cooperated fully. The only misstep, literally, was that Rowan walked through an ancient soggy dog mess when I took him into a nearby field. I didn't notice it until after we had returned to the car and he had stepped across the front seats. Fortunately we had paper toweling and water in the car, but even so, it took about forty-five minutes to wash off the seats and wash Rowan's paw, during which time all three couldn't decide whether they were being reprimanded or if I had come up with some sort of new game.

The final week before the end of that second phase turned out to be a real test for all of us. First was Molly's heat period. During most of those three weeks she again became Molly Meek while the other two remained close to unmanageable. We kept Molly confined to the two rooms at the top of the stairs, my study and a bedroom, and her pants stayed on except when she went outside. She didn't seem to mind all that much. The two males had the rest of the house, and as usual they mostly growled at each other. Rowan insisted on being Top Dog and became so demanding of me that I had to speak to him sharply.

The real trial, though, especially for Pat, was that right at the worst time of Molly's heat period I experienced two days of excruciating pain that led to Doctor Denise's meeting us in the emergency room of the local hospital. Half a day was spent with the medical crew testing for everything they could think of until, by the end of the day, they decided that it might be a pretty good idea to check out the gall bladder. And that was it. The duct was completely blocked, and so it had decided to give up the ghost. They hurried me off to a hospital room and dripped things into me that got rid of the pain and made me feel really good. Then the next morning I was wheeled into the operating room for surgery. The doctor and anesthetist both acted very serious, and while more things were dripped into me, two nurses gazed at me, one of them very motherly and compassionate, and I hoped that if I didn't make it, someone like her would be there to greet me on the other side. I did make it, though, and came to in the recovery area. They wheeled me back to the hospital room for another day, and then they allowed Pat to take me home. I learned later that the operation had been performed in the nick of time, just before the gall bladder would have gone all *blooey* and created a really serious condition.

During that whole time Pat had to look after all the dog needs—feeding, sorting out how to get them outside separately to do businesses since Molly was in heat, and drying them off during periods of steady rain and drizzle. She also had to drive—and at night, too—a "new" old car she had never driven before, and during the day of surgery on August 1 the dogs had to be left unattended and separated for over ten hours. Fortunately they acquitted themselves well, and Pat assured me that they had had no accidents and that nothing had been chewed up.

When I arrived home the next afternoon, feeling much the worse for wear, the two males were still so assertive that they had to be shut in the back room, and for a while I didn't really like them all that well. With Molly it was different. She was still Molly Meek, either because of her condition or because she knew I wasn't well. She stayed in the study with me for large portions of the following days and nights as I recovered from the surgery and the effect of the things that had dripped into me, and whenever I lay down she curled up on the bed with me. No matter how restless I became or how often I had to readjust myself, she'd look up to make sure that everything was all right. Her staying by me and becoming Nurse Molly made it difficult for Pat, because in the morning, when she came up to take Molly outside, Molly would refuse to leave me. That meant that I had to carefully get myself up, gingerly go downstairs, and walk outside until Molly did her business. If nothing else, the whole process did at least get me up and moving in the morning.

When the heat period passed, what had previously been normal now became slightly different. I had to be very severe when any of them, especially Rowan, tried to jump against me. My whole abdominal area was still tender, and to have a dog jump against it when I was standing up or try to walk on it when I was lying down could have been damaging. I also found that I couldn't endure their barking as well as before, so I ended up swatting the floor with rolled-up newspaper much more often. I was grateful for the large fenced-in areas that now allowed them to cut loose, run about, and explore on their own until I was mended.

By that fall the basic factors in their personality and physical growth were complete. Rowan stayed close when I let him, and he was jealous whenever either one of the others, especially Liam, was held or fussed over. If they came over to be noticed, he'd come over too and body-block them out of the way. Even so, he was easily distracted, so that if the others caused a commotion or barked at something, Rowan would go running off briefly and then come running back. Napping was difficult because he now ran upstairs and then back down and then back up and so on. He was also the energetic, clumsy one who became rough when playing, either biting or pawing too hard or crashing around and not knowing when to stop. We realized that at this point we had to understand it as part of his makeup and learn how to deal with it, just as we had done with various members of our center group.

Even though Liam was the most independent of the three, he became more attached to both of us. If I held him when visitors arrived, he was quiet and interested, but if I let him down, he was noisy. Without exception everyone who saw all three still thought that he was the cutest thing they had ever seen. Whenever he no longer wanted to be feisty and independent, he assumed his poor helpless little dog pose and just had to be picked up.

Molly was still the one who for me seemed to have the most varied character. Rowan might be Loyal Friend, and Liam might be Cute Little Guy, but Molly was still Molly, at various times Molly Meek, Momma Molly, Molly Queen of the Jungle, Dopey Molly, or Bat-Eared Molly. She didn't have the long, elegant collie-type coat of the other two, but had the thick, shorter coat of a border collie. While the two males were jealous of each other, neither one was ever jealous of Molly or of the attention she received.

All three had also finally become dependably housebroken. They took a last serious trip outside right after their supper and maybe accepted an invitation to wet just before we headed up, but that would be it until we all arose in the morning, when they would go outside and wet with great relief.

(10/6/96) If you were Liam, you would every now and then trot from room to room with a sock in your mouth trying to get someone to play with you. Perhaps that's something you've thought about doing, so I thought you'd like to know that Liam does it too.

(1/2/97) Molly is now getting ready to go into heat, which means we'll again have to have her wear britches and sanitary pads for two or three weeks. Denise, our friendly family doctor, once fell about in helpless laughter upon seeing Molly in her britches and hearing about the sanitary pads. I patiently explained why she was wearing them, as though a woman doctor had never heard of such things before, but every now and then she would stop me, make a few rude comments, and then fall about all over again. That's the kind of family doctor we have.

(1/29/97) It was during Molly's summer heat period that my gall bladder decided to go all funny, and our doctor practically frogmarched me to the hospital and as much as told me to Sit and Stay. In about two weeks Molly will again Turn Critical. I may or may not have anything else go all funny enough to have to be removed.

After my operation the surgeon had told me that it would take six months before I'd feel recovered. He was right, and after a careful summer and fall, all the late-season jobs were completed so that by the end of the following January we were ready to move back to the smaller front space until spring.

The dogs had become thoroughly acclimated to their larger outdoor area. After every snowfall I headed out back with the snow shovel to generally knee-deep snow and cleared out seven intersecting circular passageways through a good part of the whole back area. Molly was the one who now ran like the wind, and the guys had to try their best to keep up with her. Liam, the clever one, discovered that he could take short-cuts through the mazelike corridors and head her off. After the first straight-out run through the corridors, they would play "find me-chase me-chase you" without prejudice. When they were ready to come back inside, they'd be all smiles. It made all that shoveling worth the effort.

They still barked wildly whenever anyone arrived, but they eased back to general wariness more quickly. Once the visitor was settled in, Liam and Molly simply walked around and sniffed while Rowan stayed close to me, but any sudden movement by the visitor elicited panic barking. They were, though, responding better to my commands to stop, and it looked as though Rowan and Liam were getting over that bossy who-is-top-dog phase. In early October we had guests that stayed for several days, and after the first little while, the dogs more or less accepted the newcomers so that their brief barking of the first morning or two gave way to wary acceptance.

Even with that ongoing wariness of visitors and mutual jealousy, the two males had become much more likeable over the year. They showed a greater sense of caring and a greater willingness to be members of a pack of five.

Our days developed a comfortable rhythm. Pat was the first one up, and the three stayed with me when she went down-stairs. After a suitable time they urged me to get up too. Liam had learned to put his front paws on my shoulder and stare at me while Rowan nosed my face. If I spoke to them or moved in any way, they all wiggled and tried to get me to play. That's when Molly would join in, growling and making playful lunges toward me. By then I'd arise and they'd think, "We did it! We did it!" All four of us then headed down the stairs, and the dogs greeted Pat as though they hadn't seen her in a long, long time. Then I'd take them to their small outside pen to tend to business. When they were all back in, we'd all sit together on the couch and watch the morning weather report on TV. After I fed them, they'd go out again to wet, and once back inside they'd hang around companionably while Pat and I worked. At noon they had lunch and went out again. Once back, they spent the afternoon roughhousing with each other all over the house and out back. Late in the afternoon they'd go out again, then urge me to feed them, and then go out still again. During the evening they joined us on the couch while we read or watched a movie. I sometimes had a silly session with them, such as getting down on all fours, growling, lunging toward them, and then crawling away in mock terror. They really enjoyed that. Pat often retired first, and Liam usually joined her on the bed. Molly now frequently headed upstairs, too, but Rowan always stayed close by me. If Molly decided to remain downstairs, she soon insisted that I go to bed too. When I did, all three would then find their spots on the bed and curl up for the night. None of the routine was mindless, and there would be all kinds of activity in between with much variation, but the pattern offered a framework for each day.

Molly had been developing a more abstract sensitivity. We first noticed it with the pennywhistle. She'd go bonkers at its sound and would run to me and leap about whenever I played it, so I decided to try an experiment. When she was upstairs by herself in my study and we were downstairs in the living room, I picked up the pennywhistle and mimed playing it without making a sound. Molly came rushing downstairs, hurried over to me, and leapt about. She continued to do that at other times when she'd be out of sight in another room, including several times when I only made believe I was even holding the pennywhistle.

On one occasion I had to be away overnight to attend a family wake and funeral about six hours away. The dogs were, of course, bewildered that I wasn't at home with them, and Pat said that all three spent the two days mostly moping. I started back in the late morning, and on the way I left the thruway and went into Hanover for about an hour to shop at the food co-op and then stop at the Dartmouth Hopkins Center for a coffee and fries to go. After I arranged everything carefully on the seat beside me, I munched my way back over the bridge and up the road. During that hour in Hanover the dogs acted outraged, as if to say, "He's not on his way anymore!" By the time I did get back on the thruway, they settled down, as though thinking, "There, that's more like it." Then about half an hour from home I ran into a wet, slippery snow squall, and again they reacted, this time pacing about in a very worried manner. When I finally did arrive home, all three were of course delirious with joy. That's probably why they kept telling me "You're home! You're home!" for nearly an hour and all wanted to be held at once.

(2/10/97) Molly is this very minute at the high tide of her heat period. Molly stays in my upstairs study with a double barrier between her and the guys except for the times when I carry her past them and let her out all by herself in the enclosed outdoor area. When the guys go out, they head directly for the spot where Molly has wet. What usually happens is that one buries his nose in the yellow snow while the other pees all over that one's face. Then they exchange places and go through the same thing all over again. It took me several days (which tells you something) to realize that I could solve the problem if I let them out one at a time.

(3/3/97) The dogs feel the glimmerings of spring. Now that Molly's heat period is over, they're giving in to cabin fever and are

ready to leap and cavort in the tall fresh grass. They hadn't been on any car trips since November, but the other day we took them on their first end-of-winter ride all the way to the Grand Union. They enjoyed it, mostly, but I still had to remind them that they didn't have to bark at every living thing that came within fifty feet of the car.

In spite of their restlessness, the shelties are back even more so to their sweet selves, at least when nobody else is around. Pat says one problem is that they're now so bonded to me that if I'm out anywhere for more than a few minutes, they huddle near her and tremble. Then when I return they all go out of their minds and wiggle and howl and all want to be noticed at exactly the same instant.

Actually, what they do is they run about and bark at things. It's like a children's story: "Oh chair, chair, he's home! Look, table, look! He's here, he's here! Come, rug, come join us in our dance of delight!"

(3/17/97) *We took the dogs in the car last week to the Grand Union, but we had also put two full bags of bottles in the back to leave at the redemption center. On the way, I had to brake suddenly, and both bags tipped over with an impressive crash of bottles, all of which tumbled all over the back of the car. The dogs decided then and there that it was the end of the world and all tried to get with us in the front seat at exactly the same instant. It made for a car ride unlike any other we've had for a long time, and now whenever I put my coat and boots on and mention car, they all shiver and slink away.*

(4/5/97) *The three wee beasties enjoy the wet, sloppy snow a lot more than we did, or do. They also enjoy any excuse whatsoever to run about the huge fenced-in area out back. It's a joy to watch them frisk and frolic about, full of smiles and wiggles.*

(5/26/97) *You will notice that I'm not going on and on about how really cute, loyal, and loveable the three dogs are. I figure that it's something you already know. We find it interesting that when we're out somewhere with them in the car and people pass by and they defend the whole area like crazed fanatics and we try to apologize, how many people nod reassuringly and say, "I know; I had a sheltie once." We note that they always indicate that they once had a sheltie and not that they have one now. I can't imagine why, because they're so cute, loyal, and loveable, but Pat indicates that she sort of knows what they mean.*

(7/1/97) The three shelties continue to do well and to add much joy to each day. That doesn't mean they're without faults, but any faults pale next to their virtues. Molly, ever the restless one, still runs to the door and barks furiously whenever anyone dares to pass the house on either side of the street or when a car slows down anywhere nearby. I tried to discipline her by putting her on a leash and keeping her close by me. She made it clear, however, that being on a leash was really neat. The two guys then tormented me by leaping about, saying Me! Me next! My turn! Yesterday I broke down and gave each of them equal time on the leash, and they were overjoyed. So much for punishment.

The dogs just told me they took a vote and now we all need to go outside. That's what happens when you try for democracy in the pack.

Six months passed, and we reached day 1,001. When we drove down to Northfield the next day to the annual quilt show the dogs were in the car from about 7:00 until about 5:00 and had only one short walk to wet about noon. They behaved extremely well, not barking at people walking by and not putting up a fuss when I left them for a forty-five-minute walk by myself. On the way home they were restless and did bark at people whenever we stopped anywhere, but it had been a long day for them. At home Molly still led the pack in barking at any commotion, and although she came whenever I called her, she sometimes gave a little half-howl of protest on the way.

We had made it through nearly three years, during which we spiraled from periods of deep despair to other periods of even deeper admiration, affection, and joy, and all three shelties had weathered the efforts of two bumbling, well-meaning humans to train them up within a confined environment. Our errors weren't like theirs, because we were already housebroken and had long since learned not to howl at visitors, and while we finally did train them to be our companions, they did a pretty good job of training us to be fellow pack members with them. It was the end of the first cycle, not the end of the journey, and we had all survived it and had become a small group of loyal companions who were now ready to face together whatever the next cycles would bring.

The early training days had now been completed and if this process had indeed mirrored a retreat, we had now progressed successfully through discomfort, silliness, boredom, rejection, and doubt. Next came what we thought was the stage of contentment.

8

Maturity

DURING THE next eight years things progressed smooth-
ly. All those difficulties of housebreaking and training had
been resolved, and all three shelties had now developed their
unique characteristics and become loyal, affectionate, loving
companions to us and to each other. We enjoyed that time,
not realizing that we were still in training and that the final
stages of retreat—service, acceptance, and breakthrough—
still lay ahead.

When we now took them out back, Rowan and Molly were
the ones who especially played together with mock attacks
and counterattacks. Whenever Molly took after him, Rowan
ran with a big smile as if to say, "Look! Look! She's chasing
me!" In the evening, if we sat in the living room, Molly settled herself on a folded blanket next to the couch, Rowan
curled up against my foot, and Liam jumped up to find a
comfortable spot on the couch with us.

One thing that continued to upset Rowan was the sound
of thunder, and if he heard it during the night, even when a
storm was still far off, he'd snuggle up close to me and tremble. Liam and Molly, however, ignored storms completely,
although whenever a really severe one passed over us, Molly
would wake up and look annoyed.

Although Rowan was the one who still stayed the closest
to me, Molly was the one who now claimed me as her own.
I recall that on one occasion our doctor, Denise, stopped by

for a visit, and I had to pick Molly up to stop her barking. For the full time of the visit in the living room, Molly remained seated at full alert on my lap and stared fixedly at Denise with a look that said, "He's mine!"

During September of '97 the five of us took another trip to Maine, and we all behaved ourselves really well. I could now take the dogs out one by one, often without their leashes, and follow them while they strolled down Ellen's driveway, did whatever they needed to do, circled around the big barn at the foot of the drive while sniffing everything, and returned up a tractor path to the cottage. We did use harnesses and leashes, though, whenever we walked down the side of the hill on the one-lane dirt road that led to the dock, and we made sure they were firmly attached when we sat far out over the water and observed the tide and the play of light all the way to the islands. We took them as usual to Mount Desert Island and our favorite spot at Acadia National Park, Otter Point, where they looked forward eagerly to their treks in harness along the seaside trail. We traveled around the island, as usual visiting all the used book stores, ending up with several boxes of books we both decided we really needed, and Pat buying enough material in fabric shops to make dresses that she decided she really needed. While we were in Bar Harbor, not to be outdone, I bought something I really needed, too, which in that case happened to be a didgeridoo. As near as I could tell when we left the store, I was the only person in all of Bar Harbor who happened to be carrying a didgeridoo at that particular time, and people we passed glanced uneasily in my direction before quickly looking away.

Back at the cottage, after we gave the didgeridoo a really good scrubbing, I tried my skill with it and got it to make a rude noise you don't really want to know about. All three dogs leaped to my rescue. After our return home I didn't play the didgeridoo all that much, because my skill seemed to be firmly fixed at the rude noise stage that alerted all three dogs to full rescue mode. Whenever I put it to one side the dogs knew I was safe, but even so, they'd still eye it with suspicion and remain close by just in case.

Several weeks later the dogs either came down with a minor bug or discovered a new way to get our attention. First Rowan threw up in the middle of the night on the floor next to the bed. Then two nights later Molly used tremendous effort to make it onto the bed just before she let loose. Then a couple of nights later Liam likewise made it onto the bed just in time. So for a brief period we became accustomed to doing major clean up and laundry in the middle of the night. Fortunately, after they had each finished putting their new technique to the test, all three either recovered or had the good sense to think about it and decide that maybe they ought to work out other ways to get our attention.

(12/18/97) I'm typing this rather slowly because Liam decided that he really, really needed to be held. He has mastered the art of looking pathetic, so I'm holding him while practicing my one-finger typing skills.

Last week the weather was cloudy, snowy, and chilly. This week it's been sunny with an occasional rise to the upper thirties. The three beasties are bored silly, and every now and then they gang up on me and insist that I do something with them, even if it's just crawling around the floor and growling. I've done a fair amount of crawling and growling, and the dogs seem to like it. It is not, however, what one usually thinks of as a meaningful activity.

(2/25/98) We're delighted to hear that you now have another dog, and a sheltie at that! We know without even asking that it displays the best qualities of its full ancestry and is by now an indispensable member of the household and is keeping you healthy and alert. Let me add, though, that I sort of think you should have held out for three sheltie puppies, but maybe you don't really want to be that healthy and alert.

A month later we learned more about the value of veterinary care and the natural healing power of dogs as a result of an occurrence between Rowan and Liam. During one of our center classes, when Molly was in heat, we kept her downstairs with us while the two males stayed upstairs behind a gate. We had asked the group to enter through the store doors, remove their coats, pass through the store, come down those four steps to the house part, and then sit and stay in the big living room. Partway through the class one of the members had to go back to his car for some reason and went out through the store doors.

The inside store door was outfitted with a buzzer arrangement that sounded loud and clear throughout the house until the door was fully opened, at which time it shut itself off. It did, however, have one flaw that usually made no difference. Whenever the door was opened only partway, the buzzer would become jammed and continue to buzz even if the door were again closed. Whenever that happened, the door had to be reopened all the way and then shut, but that was something the center member didn't know. He opened the door partway, and the buzzer began its steady buzz as he went to his car. When he returned, he tried to figure why it wouldn't shut off and decided it had something to do with the outside door, which he then opened and closed and examined carefully, but the buzzing continued and by then Rowan and Liam, confined upstairs, were barking wildly. Another member of the class rose and told me not to worry because he would check out the problem. The buzzer continued to buzz, and finally I went over. By then they were both working on the outside door, trying to plumb its secrets. It took me about one second to open the inside door all the way to stop the buzzing, and we all had a good laugh.

When we returned, I decided to check on Rowan and Liam. When I reached the top of the stairs, I saw blood sprayed everywhere, a bewildered Liam huddled in the hallway, and an equally bewildered Rowan looking out from the bedroom. I quickly checked Liam and found that one ear had been ripped apart from near the base to the tip, the result of a major fight. Ears bleed profusely, and Liam had evidently been shaking his head for some little time. I cleaned up the spray of blood, carried Liam downstairs, and asked Pat to call our long-suffering veterinarian, Doctor Susan. She wasn't terribly upset by the incident but said that she'd be right over. I took Liam to the back kitchen, sat on a stool, and held him while Pat took over the rest of the class, which continued as though nothing whatsoever had happened.

About half an hour later Susan showed up with her kit, cleaned up the ear, shaved some of the hair away, and then used some sort of medicated glue to hold the two sides of the ear together. She assured us that Liam would soon be all right again and that the two sides would reconnect so well that we wouldn't be able to tell that anything had ever happened. She was, of course, right, and after the hair grew back and pushed the glue out of the way, the ear was indeed as good as new.

From the experience we learned several things. First, we were reminded that allopathic medical attention could be an enormous help to the natural power of self-recovery an animal has when injured. And second, we were also reminded that even though some people might be really good center members, it didn't necessarily mean that they would have a clue about some things we took for granted, like buzzers on doors and who only knew what else.

(3/16/98) After weeks and weeks of seriously thinking about it, Molly went into heat and is now almost but not quite over it. I think the most critical period (no pun intended) has passed, because the two guys are today ever so slightly less hysterical. For the last several nights I've had to stay downstairs with them and block the way to the upstairs, where Molly lurks. The guys mostly have spent the nights mourning the absence of Molly, a state that they have told me about frequently. In fact, the first morning, when I let them out into their penned-in area about five thirty, they just stood in the middle of the yard and howled

their sorrows to a cold, indifferent universe. I took them right back in, though, because I didn't think that all that many of our neighbors would be sympathetic to their state at that hour.

During the following August and September the stretch of road in front of our house was being improved, and the dogs didn't like it one bit. Machinery and workmen appeared during the early hours and went at it until late afternoon. Throughout each day the dogs brought every single funny noise and strange person out there to our attention, and there were an awful lot of funny noises and strange people. During lunch hour, when all was calm, they would remain poised so that they could let me know right off when things started up again.

We also had a bossy chipmunk that took over the window feeder, glared through the window, and told us a few things for our own good whenever he decided he wanted something to eat, which was most of the time. When we put seeds out, we needed to be careful, because he was so tame that we wouldn't have put it past him to run up an arm and come into the house, and we suspected that the dogs would have had some trouble keeping track of a disoriented chipmunk rampaging through the house. When we put sunflower seeds on the ledge and shut the sliding window, Molly stared out and closely monitored every move of the chipmunk, just in case the window happened to slide open when we weren't around.

In addition to that chipmunk and those road improvements, all three had to keep track of a neighbor black cat that deposited itself in the middle of a large spread of ostrich ferns by our small pond and intimidated the wildlife. Whenever Molly saw him through the window, she let us know in some detail that he was there, that he should leave, and why was it always up to her to stay on guard. Liam made it clear that he was ready to take on the cat single-handed, but he always said that. Day after day he kept telling us that he'd take on the big, noisy road machinery single-handed, too, if we only had the good sense to let him at it.

As time went on the appeal of afternoon naps increased. The three companions saw to it, though, that I didn't fritter away too much of my time lazing about. I could be resting comfortably, and then after just so long all three dogs would leap onto the bed, climb all over me, and sniff my face with their wet, gooey noses. If I protested, they sprang to attention, smiled and wiggled, went into game mode, and leaped and cavorted all over me. Quite often I would then decide that nap time was over.

Our center classes had now reached a mellow stage, and attendees were now more willing to contribute ideas and share their experiences. During previous years Pat and I had focused on ways to have the students adapt to the material, but by now, with our more relaxed approach, we were more focused on ways to have the material adapt to the students. Our helpers at this stage were, as before, the three beasties. When Molly was on her leash, she was docile, and so during classes she stayed by my chair while I kept her leash on my lap. Liam would be uneasy for a while but then wander off a little way from my chair and stretch out for a good snooze. Rowan stayed near Pat, who kept a firm grip on his leash. When anyone arose or when the class was taking a break, Molly and Rowan rose to attention, as though daring anyone there to do anything, even though Liam would simply look up, check things out, and return to his snooze.

In February of 2000 we had a heavy snowfall, followed by a heavy snowfall, followed by yet another heavy snowfall. It was close to hip-deep, and I had to shovel those intersecting passageways all over the backyard so that the dogs could go out, have a good run, and take care of themselves. As always, I shoveled lots of alternate paths so that they could explore new routes and hide from each other. The snow was, of course, much higher than they were, so as soon as they entered the maze of passageways, they disappeared. They soon discovered ways to stay out of sight whenever I went looking for them, too, and they thought that was really neat. The downside of the snow was that it built up on the roofs, making it pretty noisy during subsequent warm spells when great portions of it came crashing down at odd hours of the day and night. It didn't bother us particularly, but the dogs were convinced that there was something out there that wasn't very nice and was trying to get in. They could have been right.

During the following year, on Christmas Day of 2001, a frightening incident occurred. As usual we had arisen, opened presents, and fed and exercised the dogs, although we had to be cautious because Molly was again in heat. During late afternoon, after darkness had set in, I took the dogs out to the large enclosed area. First I removed Molly's britches and let her go out by herself until she let me know that she was quite done and it was time to go back in. Then I let Rowan and Liam out. They first checked all the places Molly had been, and I left them alone for an instant while I went back inside to check something. When I went back out, they were nowhere to be seen. I walked the paths, but they weren't there. I checked the snow near the paths until I found their footprints, which headed toward the fence. It was when I arrived at the fence that I discovered the opening where two posts had separated and left a space just wide enough for small dogs to go through. Beyond it were dog footprints, but no dogs were in sight.

I went back to the house, alerted Pat, and returned to the footprints to see where they led. They continued to the neighbor's driveway, but beyond that they couldn't be seen. I ran down the driveway, along the sidewalk, and around to the front of our house. Huddled by the front door and looking very worried was Liam. We took him inside and I went out again, first back up the neighbor's driveway and then on through the snow up the hill and through the woods behind us to the road at the top, calling "Rowan!" all the way. There was no sign of him. I continued down that road to the north where, about a long block later, it turned and went back down the hill to the main street. Then I ran down side streets and back, still calling, before returning to our house. We alerted our neighbor, who was the local sheriff, and he told us what contacts to make in case Rowan was found and reported, and he and his wife also walked out to search the immediate area. I went back out and searched to the south, still calling, while Pat took the car and looked even further down side streets. I found nothing, but on one of the streets near a large cornfield, Pat asked a group of people on snowmobiles if they might have seen him. No, they hadn't, but they had spotted what looked like a fox that ran away from them across the large cornfield. Pat had the feeling that the animal they had seen could well have been Rowan.

Our worry intensified because we knew that Rowan was fearful of other people, that everything new and different frightened him, and that he had on absolutely no identification, not even a collar. We tried to reconstruct what Rowan must have done: run with Liam to the main street, been spooked by cars and run off blindly, totally lost and disoriented, while Liam returned home. We searched in vain for a long time, and then Pat dowsed to drive south on the main street. We headed that way with Pat driving while I tried the best I could to check the fields and yards we passed in the dark. There was no sign of Rowan or of any other living creature. Three miles later we turned around and headed back.

We came back to about a mile from our house, where a steep bank sloped down to the cornfield, and there, ahead of us in the high beams of the headlights, standing in the middle of the road, was Rowan. We braked in front of him and I leaped out from the passenger side while Pat opened the door on the driver side to warn any cars behind us to stop. I picked Rowan up as he gratefully relaxed into my arms, and he simply lay there as we completed our journey home, nearly four hours after he and we had left it.

Afterward I realized that our discovery of Rowan had to be more than simple coincidence. We had silently prayed that Rowan would be okay, that we would find him, and that he would know we were on our way so should try to come to where we would be. There had been no other reason for him to leave the wooded area, cross the barren, open corn field, climb the bank, and then stand in the middle of a well-traveled road on his own. According to my dowsing, it was Sean and Brigit, our beloved but long-deceased collies, who had responded to Pat's message and had been able to contact Rowan and direct him to the roadway where he would meet us at precisely the right moment. In any event, we knew that somehow or other he had indeed been directed where and when to go and at what instant to step onto the road when the car approaching at that moment would be ours.

From then on we no longer took for granted any part of our relationship with the three beasties, and we now knew, as we had suspected, that just as we were still connected with our collies, we were also connected with the shelties at a much more profound level than we had thus far realized. We were grateful for being brought to that understanding, but later we were equally grateful that we had been given four more years to experience Rowan's lively and loyal presence.

(7/23/03) Molly is now over her heat period, which is a great relief to all of us. Even though Molly is almost nine, she can still put the other two in a tizzy, which is what we had here for about two weeks. Now that the guys are back to normal along with Molly, they are all again gooder than good. Her main job now is to reassert her authority, which she is doing really quite well. Yesterday afternoon, when I thought I'd nap for a bit, Molly jumped on the bed, walked up the front of me, stared straight down into my face, and said, "No nap for the likes of you! Take

me outside and be quick about it!" So I took her outside. I have to go outside with them, because if I don't, they crowd around the back ramp and look back through the screen door expectantly. Then I go out and they all go happily about their business. It's no easy task to be the alpha dog.

Another serious event during Liam's mature years began when we took him on one of our yard-sale expeditions. When we returned to the car after one of the stops, Pat noticed a bit of blood on the floor of the front seat. We picked Liam up, checked him carefully, and discovered that he was bleeding from his gentleman parts. We hurried home and once more called Doctor Susan at her home. Yes, if we brought him to her she would take a look at him.

We drove to her house, and with Liam on her kitchen table she checked him over, determined the probable cause of the problem and told us that she needed a urine sample. Fortunately she had plastic sandwich bags. We took one and carried Liam to her front yard, where we set him down and followed him around, duck walking and urging him to wet. Most of what he did ended up all over our hands, but enough ended up in the bag for Susan to take to the clinic for a diagnosis. Later that day she called from the clinic and told us that he would need to take pills for two weeks. Once we drove down and got them, the challenge was to figure out how best to give the pills to Liam, who made it clear that he wanted nothing to do with them. Finally we worked it out: Pat held him; with one hand I opened his jaws, and with the other hand I popped the pill, coated with olive oil, to the back of his throat, after which I gently rubbed his throat and waited for telltale signs of swallowing. Liam did finally become accustomed to the procedure enough to stop fighting like a tiger, but we were all greatly relieved, especially Liam, when the procedure came to an end and he was once again pronounced thoroughly fit and healthy.

(6/27/04) It's amazing that our three lively shelties, all of whom act like puppies, are now all of ten years old. They are still, by the way, great company and totally loyal, playful, and affection-ate—all the things that shelties are justly praised for being, and they're still all so cute we can hardly stand it.

During those seven years of maturity that followed those three years of puppyhood and adolescence, the unique per-sonality of each of the shelties took shape.

Rowan was now fully a most faithful and loyal companion, reluctant to be out of sight of me and always by choice right by my side.

Liam was clearly the most intelligent of the three and con-tinued to be a very self-contained being, much like the piper Liam O'Flynn for whom he was named. He could, for ex-ample, know what a word was when he heard it spelled, and he could even recognize a word if he saw it written. He was, though, not much interested in doing this other than as a favor to Pat.

As for Molly, she continued to develop those characteris-tics that were uniquely hers—interested in everything, de-manding, affectionate when she chose to be, aloof at times, and thoroughly adorable, my special Molly.

Both Pat and I now loved all three of them without con-dition for their unique selves, and we continued to become increasingly grateful for their huge presence in our lives. We were now ready for the next stage, that of service and accep-tance.

9

Old Age

THE THREE shelties reached the conclusion of their middle years in 2005. By then we knew for a fact that the world contained only three breeds of dogs: collies, shelties, and others. It seemed very clear to us, and to this day we fail to understand why so many owners of others tend to differ.

At the beginning of summer Doctor Susan told us that if she had not known how old Rowan was, she would have thought he was half his age. As the summer went on, though, he began to have short bouts of coughing, which we felt may have been caused by allergies. He also began sleeping for longer periods, and when we now all went exploring in the backyard he no longer leaped up and frolicked about with his old enthusiasm. He had begun moving more slowly, too, and he kept close to me even more often, intermittently limping a bit and walking with more care. By the beginning of autumn he experienced periods of confusion even when he was on familiar ground. When we now went to the side yard for those morning or evening wets, I had to encourage him to follow me, and he would then sometimes lean against me as he tended to his plumbing.

By October he seemed much better. His temperature remained normal and his limping almost stopped. Later that month he had periods of weakness, and by the end of the month his weakness had increased. For several days he could hardly move and we did our best to keep him comfortable.

Whenever he became restless I carried him outside so that he could tend to himself. Then early one evening in mid-November, after I had taken him outside and back in, he collapsed and lay still, his gaze unfocused, and his breathing ragged. We placed him on the living room couch so that we could literally stay in touch with him. We called Doctor Susan at her home, and she said she'd be right over. Rowan then experienced a final episode of coughing, and as I held him just as I had held Sean and Brigit years earlier, I felt his heartbeat become slower and fainter until finally it ceased. Susan arrived moments after he left us.

We felt grateful as she assured us that those final episodes of ragged breathing and coughing were automatic responses and that he would not have been aware of them. She also told us her feeling that any earlier tests at the clinic would not have showed anything except that it was not this and not that. We had not expected Rowan to leave us so soon, but for whatever reasons it had evidently simply been time for him to go and join a new pack, the one that had been started by Sean and Brigit, his guides when he had become lost four years earlier.

After Susan left later that evening we placed Rowan on the floor by the couch on his favorite blanket. During this time we had kept Molly and Liam upstairs, and we now let them back down. They entered the living room cautiously and uncertainly as we led them over to the couch and invited them up. Molly stayed next to Pat and Liam stayed next to me while we all simply sat and looked at Rowan, thanking him for his years of companionship, wishing him well on his next journey, and telling him that he was welcome to come back and visit us whenever he wanted. When enough time had gone by, Liam gazed up at me and placed his paw on top of my hand. It was okay. Liam was letting me know in the best way he knew how that he felt really bad but that it was okay.

The next morning we prepared a burial place for Rowan in the side garden near our collies Sean and Brigit. After he was laid to rest, we brought Molly and Liam out and showed them Rowan's resting place, and from then on, whenever we brought them to the side yard for walks on their leashes, all four of us would stop by Rowan's special site and again wish him well.

> *(11/19/05) Thank you for your call last week. As you well know, Rowan's passing came as a severe shock to us. As was the case with Sean and Brigit, Rowan too passed on as I held him in my arms. All three passages were difficult, but Rowan's was especially so because it was so unexpected and because he had been my special buddy. I know that he's still around and is evidently willing to remain around, but there are times when the loss wells up. Pat was right when she said that his going created a great emptiness. Molly and Liam are still in the process of rearranging the balance of things, and they're trying very hard to fill the gap—they've become even more sweet and dear and loving than they've been right along. Still, though, whenever we're doing something that Rowan was always a part of (and he was a part of about everything), it's difficult. We did find a perfectly lovely photo of Rowan with the other two that captures his true self just right. We had it enlarged to poster size and it's now framed on the living room wall. It's a wonderful touchstone.[1]*

Some time had to go by before we could even partially adjust to the loss of Rowan. Liam had to assume a new role as my second-in-command, and Molly had to get used to trips to the backyard with no one to chase.

Shortly after Rowan's death our area of the Kingdom experienced a devastating windstorm that did enormous damage throughout the region and to almost every tree on our property. We had to spend a great deal of time and energy on cleanup and salvage. It made us grateful that Rowan's passing, since it evidently had to happen, had taken place before

---

1 See front cover photograph.

the windstorm so that we had been able to give him our full attention during his final days.

When winter arrived I still shoveled all those paths, and Liam and Molly still did enjoy exploring them, but it was never quite the same anymore.

By mid-March Molly again showed signs of going into heat, so she stayed with me, mostly in my study, while Pat took charge of Liam. Then in the early hours of Saturday the seventeenth Molly jumped down from the bed and vomited her previous night's meal undigested and at breakfast would not eat or drink anything. We called Doctor Susan for advice and learned that she had just returned home after an all-night trip with her family from a vacation. But after a few hours of sleep she came early that afternoon, saw Molly, and took a sample of discharge to check under a microscope, telling us that things were serious. Later she called us and said that Molly had pyometra and needed to have an emergency operation to remove her uterus and ovaries the following morning, Sunday, or she would probably not survive until Monday. Susan then came back to the house to inject fluid under the skin as preparation for the following morning's surgery. Although Molly had not shown any symptoms of any problem until that previous evening, Susan said that the condition must have been brewing for some time.

At eight the next morning Susan and Torie, her technician, met us at the clinic. I carried Molly into the operating room and held her as they started the flow of anesthetic, after which they politely asked me to leave. We waited in the reception area for nearly an hour until Susan came out and said that the operation had been successful. Susan knew we wouldn't want to leave Molly at the clinic unattended, so we waited until after Molly came out of the anesthetic, then were given instructions for regulating the IV to which she was attached, and were allowed to take her back home.

We set up a special bed for her on the floor of my study. First we put down a large, thick piece of foam, then covered it with waterproof plastic, and finally placed a folded blanket on top. We made sure that Molly was comfortable on it, and we hooked the IV unit to a nearby floor lamp. Next to Molly's bed I put down a folded comforter, a blanket, and a pillow, so that either Pat or I could remain by her night and day to check the IV unit and always be there in case she became restless and tried to get up. After everything was arranged, we carried Liam in and explained to him what we had done so that he would know what the plan was.

During the preceding years Molly had become quite fastidious about her personal habits, so even though she was now only semiconscious for days, she'd hold back on wetting as long as she could. Then out it would flow, after which I'd hold her while Pat dried her off, took up the wet coverings, and put down fresh plastic and a clean blanket.

Even with all that constant monitoring, though, things sometimes went awry. When the first IV bag was nearly empty, we felt uneasy about changing it and took Molly down to the clinic still attached to the bag so that a technician could do it for us and show us patiently how to do it ourselves. On another occasion I fell asleep and the IV bag became empty. Since we had no idea what might happen if air entered her bloodstream, we rushed her down once more to the clinic. The technician, who was waiting for us, attached a fresh bag and assured us that no harm had taken place. Susan, who was on duty, stopped in and checked Molly over, likewise assuring us that all was going well. Then several days later, when there was some sort of commotion downstairs or outside, Molly leaped up and ran toward the study door, falling over when she reached the end of the tubing that connected the IV to her forepaw. Again we rushed her down to the clinic, this time fearful that the needle had twisted and cut through her vein. Another vet took her in to the back room, and she and a technician checked the needle, which was okay, but they determined that it would be better if Molly was now taken off the IV attachment. She received a mild anesthetic, and afterward the technician told us that while they removed the needle and rewrapped the paw, Molly had "peed a ton," which we took as a really good sign.

When we returned home Molly was still groggy, but when I set her down on a grassy area in the front lawn, she did still another good wet. Once she was back inside, we let her stagger around a bit while Liam, who by now was very worried, checked her over carefully. For several more days we kept her in my study, carried her outside regularly so that she could take care of herself, and eased her back to her regular diet.

Even though those weeks were a confused time that required around the clock tending to Molly in addition to all our routine duties, we were again grateful. Thanks to the immediate attention from our vet and our subsequent ability to care for Molly at home during her recovery, we were allowed to experience over four and a half more years of companionship with a healthy, feisty, loving Molly.

(6/28/06) Liam and Molly seem to be doing all right. They continue to be super lovely, loyal, and affectionate, although Liam has one problem at meals. In the morning and evening I separate the dogs, putting Molly's plate behind the closed gate in the front room and feeding Liam in the kitchen. I hold the plate for him, removing it after every few bites so that he doesn't eat so heartily that it all comes back up. Liam has found, however, that every time I lower the plate again, there is less food on it than he can remember being there last time. This bothers him a great deal, because he knows that somewhere, somehow, someone is helping himself or herself to his food. He's always quite angry by the end of the meal.

Molly has now returned to her old self, which is a joy to see. She can once again go up the stairs without problem and jump on the bed whenever she wants. When it is bedtime, however, she likes to wait at the bottom of the stairs until I pick her up and carry her to the bedroom. Liam has caught on and often waits for me to come get him too. I think it's rather nice; Pat has no comment.

During 2008 Molly and Liam continued to be in good health for dogs now heading toward their fourteenth year. Molly snoozed more often, but at other times she could be quite puppylike in her playfulness, and she had become even more outspoken in reminding me in no uncertain terms when it was mealtime or when she really had to go out. Liam did the same, but he was less outspoken. He had come to recognize his responsibility in being Top Dog and therefore in charge of the well-being of the house, the yard, and us. The only time we usually left either of them was when we went grocery shopping, and every return home became a grand reunion.

In June we sponsored an all-day animal communication workshop in the Village Hall with a good leader from near Burlington. Everyone thought it was really worthwhile, especially Molly and Liam, who greeted us with great relief at the end of the day and had much to talk over with us.

For some time Liam had been losing hair. During a communication session near the close of the workshop, he told Pat that he felt bad about Rowan's death and wondered if it had in any way been his fault, and if Molly's pyometra had somehow been his fault too. He had noted that her coat was becoming skimpy and so had decided to give her his hair. His decision may have explained why Molly's coat had become as lush as Liam's once had been.

After that workshop Liam realized that we wanted to know more about the world he inhabited, and as a start he began to tell Pat when invisible beings were present, as our collie Brigit had done. He would get Pat's attention by pawing her gently and staring at her, and then we'd dowse who was there.

(9/5/08) Molly and Liam had their happy and healthy fourteenth birthday last month, and although they are slowing down and like to doze, they can still frolic like puppies from time to time. Liam has become a real buddy, and Molly now takes it upon herself to look after me. When Pat tries to take them out back, they don't run for the door; they run over to me to make sure I'm coming with them. When we're outside and Molly starts to head down a path, she'll stop, turn around, look at me and ask, "Well, are you coming or not?" I follow her, and then she's content.

By late November Molly and Liam were still doing okay for fourteen-year-old shelties and liked to go walkabout in the backyard and frolic about. Although Molly's eyesight and hearing were fading, she still liked to do as much sniffing as possible. During the year Liam had developed a perianal hernia, though, and also kept losing even more hair around his chest and sides. Since days and nights were turning chilly and he now had little natural protection, Pat had knitted jackets for him that slid over his head, so when I took him outside he appeared to be an animated cookie jar. Liam was also becoming a bit stiff and liked to walk and walk and walk in order to work it off. I got my exercise keeping up with him.

During the winter of 2009 our main focus increasingly had to be on Liam. I kept various paths shoveled clear out back for Molly and Liam, but I couldn't do much about the degree of cold. Molly was good about going out, doing what needed doing, and coming right back in, but in addition to his stiffness, Liam had by now lost most of his sight and hearing, too, and he sometimes became confused, so I had to stay close by to rescue him whenever he wandered somewhere and began to panic. When I now took him out back to the paths, he was apt to walk into one of the walls of snow and, when he squatted to do a business, which sometimes was difficult, he often fell over backward, so I had to always make sure he had on his harness with a leash as well as his coat.

I now let Molly in her own outspoken way say when it was time for them to go out. Sometimes 2:00 a.m. was the time to go out, but that was okay.

During February Liam began experiencing more difficulties. Doctor Susan had retired some time earlier, and he had been seeing his new vet, Doctor Kathy, quarterly for clearing his anal glands and checking on the perianal hernia for which he had been taking a daily probiotic. Other than that he had been in good general health despite his hair loss. Then over a short period his right eye started to bleed and developed a deep ulcer. His eye pressure, which had been normal, became very high, and Doctor Kathy diagnosed glaucoma. At the same time blood tests registered high for kidney and pancreatic problems. For several days in a row we took him to the clinic for fluid therapy, and from mid-February on we put him on a low-fat diet and took him to the clinic three times a week for under-skin fluid. In addition to that fluid, he now received glaucoma drops in both eyes—the other eye had started to bleed, too—and an antibiotic for the poorer eye. Liam and Molly had been eating pretty much a kidney diet but we now cut out the occasional square of Muenster cheese and treats of cornbread with butter.

By March Liam really couldn't see at all and had to be carried outside to do business. He also increasingly experienced petit mal seizures, although they seemed to lessen and his health somewhat improved. Even though it was all pretty awful for him, our dowsing indicated that it was his wish to still be with us and that we were to continue to do our best to support him.

At our request Doctor Kathy had also contacted Doctor Kim, a holistic vet in New Hampshire with whose work she was familiar and with whom we worked out other complementary steps, including homeopathy, for Liam's well-being. We now gave Liam eye drops at eleven different times day and night. At first Pat and I tried working together to give them, with Pat holding him while I administered the drops, but Liam fought it. Finally I worked out a more benevolent way. I waited until Liam was napping, then lifted his head slightly and put in the drops before he was fully awake.

Despite his condition, Liam remained determined, and we felt that he clearly still wanted to live. Even so, it was heartbreaking to see him struggle night and day to try to remain independent and maintain his dignity.

We fixed a place for him between the dining room table and the bureau in the front room—three pillows covered with a soft blanket and, by the bureau, a bolster he could lie against. When he became restless, I'd lie next to him so that he and I could literally stay in touch, and when he had to go out, I'd bundle him up, put on his harness, and carry him out back to one of the intersections in the paths. After setting him down, I let him roam to the limit he was able but stood ready to assist if he started to fall over or walk into a sidewall of snow. Sometimes when he had to squat, the harness was not enough support and I had to reach down and steady his haunches to keep him from falling over backward.

Pat prepared his small, frequent meals from scratch and kept track of the times to administer his complicated schedule of eye drops. During the night each of us took turns checking to make sure he was okay, because sometimes he'd get up, wander about, and become lost. At such times I would pick him up and hold him, sometimes for hours, until I felt him relax, and then I'd carry him back to his bed and lie down next to him with my hand on his front paw until he was asleep.

During all this time Molly continued to do the best she could to keep a close watch on Liam and on me, although I told her that I was okay and that it would be good if she could spend more time in the front room next to Liam. She understood, and from then on she spent more time near him, although she'd still leave now and then to check to make sure that I was still okay.

Two weeks previously Pat had developed a really nasty cold that, for a while, threatened to become something more serious. She spent several days in bed, or at least as much in bed as she could, given that she had to be the driver during all those times we took Liam to the clinic, had to assist in giving him his medication and keeping the schedule straight, and had to get his meals together. My time was taken up with keeping an eye on Liam, keeping the back paths shoveled (it had been snowing relentlessly), keeping the front walkway shoveled and the car shoveled out and ready, keeping the paths to the bird feeders open, and bringing in load after load of wood from the stacks in the side yard.

As we had been doing, we continued to prepare Liam's three meals every day and dowse what was appropriate each time. For his midday meal Pat now offered him cooked ground turkey, beef broth, rice, half an egg, parsnip or rutabaga or sweet potato, and kale or broccoli or another green vegetable. His evening meal continued to include finely cut up chuck roast which we also carefully dowsed, beef broth, rice, and a bit of mashed carrot and peas. In addition, each meal included a half pack of FortiFlora and an eighth of a teaspoon of the powdered Belfield vitamins, and in April we added a bit of salmon oil to his morning meal. Herbalist Rosemary Gladstar had given us information on the salmon oil she used for her own dogs, and it dowsed the best. He was also now given one tablet of FlavenZym divided over the day, with each segment wrapped in a tiny bit of American cheese. His stool, although sometimes soft, stayed within normal range.

After the snow melted and spring arrived, Liam's hair began to grow back soft and feathery and he slowly regained some of his strength. The pressure in his right eye had diminished, and now both the right and left eyes were beginning to close for good. Since he could no longer see and slept quite a bit, he had difficulty distinguishing between night and day, and so I had to stay alert to take him outside whenever he felt the urge to go. Sometimes at night, when I failed to hear him get up, he'd find his way to the living room couch, where I now slept, and ask to be taken out. We had an outside floodlight, so night or day I could carry him outside to the now dry places he was familiar with on the paths and let him wander a bit without his harness, redirecting him only if he was headed for berry bushes or complicated areas of shrubbery. If he did not tend to himself in one spot, I'd pick him up and carry him to another one, which he would then try to investigate. He let me know when he had enough, and I'd carry him into the screened back room, wipe his bottom free of any soft stool, and take him into the living room, which he had pretty well committed to memory by now.

(From Pat's e-mail to Doctor Kim and Doctor Kathy, 6/1/09) After Liam gets up in the night it sometimes takes hours to settle him back down. He gets up from his bed again (and sometimes yet again) and barks to be held, which Dick does. But we hope eventually that we all will again be able to sleep through the night. Liam seems each day more sturdy and now gets around the house better on his own and, once he knows a meal is under-way, waits patiently in the kitchen for it.

Liam slept quietly without any signs of distress during the day, but from midnight until six in the morning he had be-gun to be more and more restless, walking about and want-ing to be held. Sometimes he shook and then I'd hold him until he became quiet. During the night of June 5 I was up with him from midnight until six, taking him outside to wet and trying to quiet him down. He would relax, I'd put him on his bed, and he would get up again, restless. By the night of the solstice, however, he entered a new phase of calmness and generally slept from 7:00 or 8:00 p.m. until 2:00 or 3:00

a.m., at which time he would ask to go out. We'd give him a bite to eat when he came back in, and he'd sleep without pacing until the morning meal.

(From an e-mail to Doctors Kim and Kathy, 6/26/09) Liam continues to grow hair. Only a few bare spots remain, especially behind the shoulders, although fuzz is beginning there too. Interestingly, the spots that first lost hair—his chest and to either side of it—are filling in well.

By July 3 nearly all Liam's previously hairless areas had at least a slight covering of soft fuzz and he began to look a bit like a soft, cuddly toy.

(From an e-mail to Doctor Kim, 7/7/09) When Liam is outside, he does more roaming now than he has in the past. After a while, though, he will become uncertain about where he is and send me "pick me up" signals. And inside, when he's hungry or has to go out, he has developed a really authoritative bark!

(10/7/09) As you know, our lives have been significantly affected by the requirements of tending to Liam's needs. We don't mind, but out daily routines are not what they were ten or more months ago. Liam's condition is now stabilized, so that we get him up, fix his breakfast while he paces about reminding us that he's hungry, take him outside, give him eye drops, take him to the vet clinic three times a week, keep his bed comfortable, take him outside during the day, fix his supper while he paces about reminding us that he's hungry again, take him outside, give him more eye drops, and settle him down until he gets up between one and two in the morning to be taken outside, then resettled until about four in the morning, when he has to go outside again and is then wide awake and paces off and on until breakfast about seven. During it all Molly continues to be an absolute angel, keeping track of Liam and his two caregivers the best she can with her limited hearing and fading eyesight.

Throughout Liam's difficulties we continued to dowse that he did not want to be put to sleep, that he still wanted and was intended to be here.

By early fall Liam's hair had regrown so that he was covered with a thick, soft, and even more cuddly layer of downy fur. Our schedule continued as it had been since the previous winter, with three trips a week to the vet clinic, regular consultations with both vets, and around-the-clock care.

With his renewed strength and his determination to be the one to have the final say about things, Liam now wandered the house more than he had, as though he were seeking something, perhaps now feeling it was time to find a way out of his present condition but on his own terms.

On November 16 he found that way out.

(From Pat's Christmas letter, 12/23/09) Most of the year has circled around the needs of our beloved sheltie Liam. The previous year he had some hair loss around his chest and a perianal hernia was discovered, but otherwise he seemed well, and the local allopathic vet thought so, just putting him on probiotics. But in February of this year more problems became evident. First one eye bulged scarily with severe glaucoma, and the other eye followed, a severe kidney problem developed, and he gradually lost most of his body hair. We began giving Dorzolamide generic eye drops twice a day to reduce the pressure. A holistic vet consulted by phone sent homeopathic phosphorus twice and also prescribed a whole-body enzyme. Later an herbalist suggested the particular salmon oil we dowsed was best. At the animal hospital Liam was given under-skin fluids three times a week to assist his kidneys. He became blind but otherwise carried on, surprising all the vets and staff by his resilience and also by his grace under pressure. Here we were happy to care for him, which meant round-the-clock, taking him out when he let us know his need. Dick, his pack master since puppyhood, took on most of this, never having a night's unbroken sleep. Often Liam would need to go out several times at night, and then, if he was restless, sometimes Dick would hold him for an hour or so. I did what I could around the edges and tried to make new and enticing meals, although eventually Liam preferred to return to as close to his old pattern of eating as he was allowed.

He was doing well. The blood tests were showing steady improvement. But suddenly on November 15 he started to have a little cough and slight trouble in breathing. On Monday, November 16, he went for his usual fluid under the skin—after a more than usually restless night and for the first time not eating his breakfast with the salmon oil that he loved—and one of the vets found that he had a very little fluid in the lungs and said that if he didn't eat dinner and breakfast the next day he would suggest that he should come in for an X-ray. There was no indication of urgency; Liam's breathing seemed better at home and he slept quietly and then ate his dinner. But shortly thereafter he became restless again and quickly died, cradled in Dick's arms, where he had spent so much time last year.

Last winter I had dowsed that Liam would regrow his fur (he did) and would be with us at least into August. As usual, he gave us more. I dowsed that he could have lived into the spring but that it would not have been good for him. And we, and especially Dick, were so extremely tired that, although sudden and a shock, we have come to recognize that it was to the highest good that Liam left when he did. We were able to bury him just before the ground froze. And we have been cheered to have his spirit return several times already, full of joy in being able to see again and to romp with our other dogs in the spirit realm.

What was it all about? Certainly the awareness of Liam's grace under pressure and his opportunity to feel our love in action. And probably partly to have the allopathic and holistic vets working together, accepting our frequent dowsing input and also the herbalist's suggestion. We have had notes from all those concerned, for they all were impressed by Liam.

With Liam gone and with no other siblings present, Molly was now able to focus her undivided attention on me, just as I was now able to focus my attention on her. We checked her condition with Doctor Kathy at the clinic, and a test showed that she now had a serious heart-valve problem. From then on, except for brief trips to the grocery store, I was with her night and day. We continued holding center classes, and I would hold Molly as we greeted each arrival and then carry her into the living room and set her down next to my chair. The group understood the situation, accepted Molly as one of the members, and went out of their way to add to our group discussions.

All during that following winter I kept the paths shoveled in the backyard, and several times each day Molly and I went out to explore them. With her failing eyesight and her diminished hearing, she sometimes became a bit confused, but even so, if she were the one in the lead, she'd go partway down one of the paths, then stop and turn to make sure that I was following. After we finished checking out all the paths, she usually chose to stay in the lead and take me back to the house.

This ritual continued through the spring and summer, even though her fading vision still could cause her to become bewildered. That's when I'd be the one to get her attention, start going down one of the paths, and then wait for her to catch up. If I stopped, she'd move ahead of me and, as before, would stop, turn around, and wait until she was sure I was following. Sometimes she'd ask to be taken on a scenic tour, which meant that I'd pick her up and carry her around the paths while bringing her attention to various points of interest. Then I'd set her down so that she could once again lead us both back home.

(E-mail to Doctor Kathy, 8/9/10) Molly started the FortiFlora each day on 7/23, as you suggested. . . . She seemingly has been doing well except that during hot muggy weather (of which we have had so much) she sometimes eats just part of one of her two meals a day, other days both meals. (We have stopped the noon bagel snack in the mostly hot weather; both morning and night she has been getting the rice, beef pot roast, carrot and pea meal, with the Belfield vitamins, FortiFlora, and E in the morning and Belfield vitamins and salmon oil at night). When she doesn't eat all of the meal, sometimes before it is ready she has had very tiny throw-ups, mostly seemingly of hunger bile. Bowel

movements and wetting have seemed normal until today, when at 10:45 a.m. she had some diarrhea that looked gummy and unpleasant—and she didn't make it to outside, though tried to.

In spite of her loose businesses, we kept Molly on her regular food, and by the middle of the month she did not have any more episodes of gummy stool. The only difference we noted was that she was eating a bit less now and would sometimes finish only a portion of a meal (usually the evening one) and then walk away. Her wetting and businesses remained okay, although she sometimes still had moments of dry retching, usually late in the evening or when it was nearly time for her evening meal.

For several weeks I had begun taking Molly on leash walks around our front yard, checking out the property line, the woodpiles, the apple tree, the bird feeders, and stopping briefly by the side garden where the other dogs had been laid to rest. After a while I could occasionally remove the leash and she'd then lead me on our rounds. If she did become uncertain, I'd go in front and she'd follow. Whenever she stopped and looked bewildered, I'd pick her up and take her on another scenic tour. Back in the house I'd sometimes urge her to join me in play, but by now she was mostly content to just wander a bit and then nap. At night she began to do what Liam had done, which was to search areas she didn't usually bother with, as though looking for something, perhaps for those who had gone before. I'd pick her up and walk around with her until she seemed relaxed and comfortable and then place her back on her bed.

During the night of August 19 she began to have difficulty in breathing, so early on the morning of the twentieth we took her down to the clinic to see Doctor Kathy. Her condition had suddenly become serious, and after she was given an injection of Lasix and a period of time on oxygen, we took her back home. She rested quietly during the day and seemed to breathe more easily, but during that night she again became restless and began to wander. I held her for perhaps an hour before placing her back on her bed in the living room. If you need me, I said, make a noise or come over to me. We exchanged a long look, and she seemed to tell me not to worry, that everything was all right.

As clearly as I could later determine, she waited until she was sure I was asleep on the couch before she quietly arose and made her way to the front room. She chose to maintain her independent nature to the end, and it was there that she began her journey to join the rest of the pack.

The next morning we carried her from the front room and placed her on the living room couch on her favorite blanket. Pat went to the screened back room so that I could say good-bye to Molly in my own way. I took out my cedar flute and, after a few moments to connect with Molly's spirit, played a last melody that tried to capture her real being and bid her farewell and safe journey. When it was completed, I again sat quietly, and Pat told me that in the silence she heard a soft, otherworldly fluted response that seemed to arise from the hillside to the east. We knew then that Molly's journey had been completed and that she was being welcomed as the final member of the pack with the four other beloved companions.

(E-mail from Pat to Doctor Kathy, 8/21/10) We have to report that Molly left us during the night.

At about 4:00 p.m. yesterday she had a good wet, and from five o'clock on her breathing eased almost to normal, so that she was resting comfortably. She got the Lasix pill about 7:30 p.m. and refused food again, went out about midnight but did not do anything, was resting and breathing comfortably again, but left us several hours later. For some time she has been more and more aware of the spirit world and of our other dogs visiting frequently from there, and I felt that she was longing for the freedom of full capacities again in that world and particularly for romping again with her litter-mate Rowan, who was the first of the three to leave at age 11.

We will miss Molly terribly, especially Dick, for whom she was his first choice and very special one. These three littermates (Rowan, Molly, and Liam) were especially "his" dogs, after his retirement from teaching, and he took the major care of them all their lives.

Molly was 16 on August 17, and people who saw her then and the next day at a class here said how fine she looked. On the nineteenth in the afternoon she began pacing and wanting to explore all around the house and yard. The not eating all or part of one of her meals we noted, but it was not unusual from time to time. During the night of the nineteenth her breathing became labored, and as you know, we called you first thing the next morning and, fortunately, you were able to see her right away yesterday. So this closing down all happened very quickly.

We are grateful for the almost 4½ years Molly Bloom had with us since her critical surgery with Susan and Torie, and for the care and help given to her since then especially by you but also by the other members of your very special staff. We thank you all for your kindness as well as care.

(Letter to center members 8/23/10) Many of you will be saddened to learn that one of our most loyal center members, our dear sheltie Molly, left this world during the early morning hours on Saturday.

One of Molly's jobs, especially during her later years, was to check each of you out when you arrived for class—or indeed even if you just dropped by for a visit—and if she wasn't quite sure about you, she would tell you about it and let you know a few things for your own good. You will recall that during classes she would often stay close to my chair and speak out if any of you made the least gesture that she knew would be out of line. Last Wednesday she apparently approved of all of you when you arrived and felt free to remain in the front room during class, confident that all of you had finally learned how to behave yourselves.

It will be some time before the great emptiness created by her passing can be filled with all the countless warm memories of her beloved presence, but we know that during future classes *she, along with her littermates Liam and Rowan, and our collies Sean and Brigit, will continue often to be present at our gatherings, watching over us and offering us their unconditional love.*

There was now a great emptiness on the physical plane, but it had helped a great deal that by the following Monday Molly was ready to join the others and pay us a visit. Now Sean, Brigit, Rowan, Molly, and Liam all return together as a pack very frequently to visit from the spirit world. So it has become a different kind of relationship but still a continuity for which we are very grateful. All these dogs, each very different, grew to become wonderful beings and friends, and we have been and still are surely blessed by their presence in our lives.

Afterword

FOLLOWING THEIR time here on earth we'd had spirit visits from Sean, Brigit, Rowan, and Liam, but it was not until Molly joined them on the Other Side that they apparently were enabled to be with us most of the time. We have made no attempt to bind them here, wanting for them, as for all those who leave the earth life, that they go on to "their next proper stage of development." But we have been given to understand that their present role is the one that is their next stage of development and that they can be here with us now almost continuously while at the same time being elsewhere too and so are not missing out on anything. Well, wonderful!

The dogs are now active as a pack of five—Sean and Brigit, the two beloved collies, and Rowan, Molly, and Liam, the three beloved shelties. They are once more all vigorous and happy, content to continue as a pack. They now act as our guides to those portions of the world that remain invisible to us, and they help us to enlarge our understanding of them. And they wait with patience for the time when we will be joining them.

Even with our great pleasure in their continued presence we had not been prepared for this whole new relationship. We have become even more aware of the deep intelligence of our dogs.

We knew that dogs in general have many senses far superior to our human ones, but we have been surprised to learn that they know a great deal more about everything than we had imagined. When we talk to our pack of five, we often ask questions in a binary mode to which we can dowse the answers, but very often they are aware of our questions before we ask and answers just spring into our minds.

For example, recently Pat tried to dowse the reason why I often experienced migraine headaches, and one day Liam told her that I needed to get special glasses calibrated to the exact distance from my usual seat for watching the TV screen, something that had not occurred to us. We did what Liam said, and the headaches significantly diminished.

The dogs are now also our ambassadors to other animals we have been asked to dowse about, and they have brought back information that we would not have thought to ask. And the communication is becoming each day easier. We had studied books, especially those by Amelia Kinkade and Penelope Smith, and knew that much could be communicated, but the dialogue now developing between our dogs and us, although still at an early stage, continues to increase. We feel that the story of this relationship is far from over, that we still are, and will continue to be, "going to the dogs."

In November of 2011 we acquired another sheltie, a nearly nine-year-old with the energy and enthusiasm of a puppy. Several weeks earlier, with permission from the pack of five, we had focused our intent, spread the word, and searched the Web. After making contact with Granite State Sheltie Rescue and talking with a volunteer, we were led to our new sheltie, Finn Cara, just as perhaps Finn was led to us. His name had been Shep, but as with our other five, we decided on an Irish name, Finn, the name of the famous hero and king of the Fianna, as well as of a number of other Finns in Irish mythology. Also we liked its resonance with Finnbheara, leader of the fairies in Connacht, and Fintan, the shape-shifter and holder of wisdom. "Cara," as in Anam Cara, means "beloved friend."

Finn is large, more like a small elegant collie. Within days he had adapted to our ways just as we had to his. In addition to his own unique qualities, he shows traits of all five of the pack. He has the friendly dignity of Sean, the sensitivity to subtle realms of Brigit, the good-buddy attitude of Rowan, the loveable bossiness of Molly, and the feisty intelligence of Liam.

As we think back about our time with Rowan, Molly, and Liam, we sometimes ask ourselves whether, if we had known at the beginning what we know now, would we still have been willing to spend those sixteen years going to the dogs? Would we still have gone through with it? Would we still be willing to go back and once again put up with all those early frustrations and later those demanding periods of care?

We recall the old understanding that it is we humans who allow dogs to grow into awareness of themselves, and we would add that it is also dogs, with their growing unconditional love and companionship, that allow people to become more human. Joseph Bruchac has written of a Native American understanding, a variation of the one regarding dogs as guardians of the Cinvat Bridge, that after you pass beyond this life you come to a log across a chasm, and on the other side, holding it steady if you have treated them well, are the dogs that have been part of your life. They continue to hold it steady as you carefully step across the log. And I like to think that they then greet you with a great commotion when you arrive safely on the other side.

When the time comes for Pat and me to take leave of this life, I find it interesting to imagine that we might well confront that log across the chasm. If so, then on its far side Sean, Brigit, Rowan, Liam, Molly, and someday Finn would watch us eagerly as they hold the log steady. Once we make our way safely across, we'd enjoy a grand reunion, and then we'd be ready to head off as the dogs began to lead us. I like to think, though, that every now and then Molly would be the one to stop, turn around, and make sure we were still there as all six of them led us on the way back home.

So would we have still gone through with it? If we had known, would we still have been willing to spend so much time going to the dogs? The story of this expanding relation-ship is far from over, but would we have started it in the first place? The answer is simple: yes, we would have. Yes, and again, yes!

Postscript

MY DEAR husband left this world unexpectedly on June 29, 2012, but after a very difficult five months that he endured with grace and his usual way of trying to learn from whatever life presented—a time during which he was also surprised and deeply touched by the love and appreciation shown to him by our current center group.

Dick and Finn Cara had become strongly bonded, and Dick's death was another hard blow for Finn, for whom this was his third home. I learned recently that Dick had asked Finn to stay with me for seven years, which he did, caring for me as I did for him, and being my loyal companion as we carried on with the center classes and our otherwise now mostly solitary retreat. Finn had many health issues, but amazed our vet Susan by his resilience. (Susan had come out of retirement after her children had grown.) Finn was beautiful and dignified, always showed grace under pressure, and was also our longest living dog—16½ years and 16 days. It is good to think of him now happy in his reunion with Dick and his meeting with the rest of the pack.

I continue to be very grateful for support from the world beyond. There must be more that I am meant to do here or to learn from whatever life will present. The press publishing this book is named for Finn Cara.

We very much appreciate the help of Cannon Labrie and Sandra Lillydahl in preparing this book for publication, and of Al Marin for his computer assistance.

Patricia C. Wright

About the Author

RICHARD DANFORTH WRIGHT (1933–2012) earned a BA from Williams College, majoring in psychology, and two MAs, including one from Middlebury College's Bread Loaf School of English. He was a lifelong student and a teacher of many different subjects, including English. He also led library reading groups for the Vermont Council on the Humanities and the Vermont Center for the Book, read widely, wrote many reviews of new books, led meditation classes for the Wellness Center of the local hospital, and as a Representative of what was then known as Sufi Order International (now the Inayati Order), for thirty years taught classes on meditation and a wide variety of nondenominational spiritual subjects at his nonprofit center.

Richard had also been a trustee of the American Society of Dowsers and an editor of their journal, *The American Dowser*. In the mid-1980s he and T. Edward Ross 2nd developed a dowsing school focused on mind reach that attracted participants with scientific and medical backgrounds from a number of countries. Richard wrote articles, gave many talks on dowsing, and chaired dowsing and consciousness symposia he and his wife organized as part of three national dowsing conventions they planned. Richard wrote two dowsing books, *The Divining Mind* with Terry Ross and *The Divining Heart* with his wife, Pat, both published by Inner Traditions International. He also wrote *Tale of the Reed: A Journey of Retreat*, published in 2019 by Finn Cara Press.

Richard had a great interest in music, played several instruments, and had been Executive Director of the North
Country Concert Association. He was very much attuned to
the natural world and took great pleasure in nature and in
the companionship of wonderful dogs.

Liam

CPSIA information can be obtained
at www.ICGtesting.com
Printed in the USA
LVHW051312280820
664255LV00007B/479